The disruption of the British party system

Manchester University Press

The disruption of the British party system

A guide to the next general election

Richard Rose

MANCHESTER UNIVERSITY PRESS

Published by Manchester University Press
Oxford Road, Manchester, M13 9PL

www.manchesteruniversitypress.co.uk

British Library Cataloguing-in-Publication Data
A catalogue record for this book is available from the British Library

ISBN 978 1 8070 7210 0 hardback

First published 2026

EU authorised representative for GPSR:
Easy Access System Europe, Mustamäe tee 50, 10621 Tallinn, Estonia
gpsr.requests@easproject.com

Typeset
by New Best-set Typesetters Ltd
Printed in Great Britain
by CPI Group (UK) Ltd, Croydon CR0 4YY

Contents

Figures

Tables

Tables

Preface

Elections are facts of political life, but party systems are not. Since the end of the Second World War in 1945, Britain has had two party systems and a third is now taking shape. The classic two-party system came back into being in 1950, when voters rejected the Liberal attempt to maintain a three-party system. The Conservative Party led by Winston Churchill and Labour led by Clement Attlee were its central figures. A hybrid three-party system was created by the 'Who governs?' elections of 1974. The electorate made the Liberal Party once again a significant competitor for votes, while the first-past-the-post electoral system maintained two-party competition for control of government. Margaret Thatcher and Tony Blair were central figures in this system.

The 2024 general election disrupted the hybrid three-party system as the two governing parties won barely half the popular vote. The aim of this book is to explain the significance of the last general election for the next one, due by 2029. It will tell us whether a new multi-party system is emerging with up to six parties and which of three parties – Labour, the Conservatives and Reform UK – are the winners and losers. Nigel Farage has made himself the central figure in the process of disruption.

In writing this book I have drawn on the experience of 19 British general elections. On election night 1959 I was off camera in the BBC television studio, using a slide rule to turn election results into percentages that David Butler could then present as a measure of the swing of the vote between two parties competing for government. In 1974 I was dividing my time between the ITN studios and *The Times*, patiently reminding journalists and audience that winning the most votes did not necessarily mean winning control of government with a parliamentary majority.

In 2024 I woke up in my home in the Scottish Highlands the morning after the election and began wondering what would follow. Would the thin ice of votes on which Labour's parliamentary majority rested harden or crack? What could Conservatives offer to the electorate that would enable them to recover from their worst defeat in history? As Reform UK supplanted Labour as the party leading in the polls, a fresh question arose: will Nigel Farage be able to institutionalise his personal appeal in a party that can fight and win a parliamentary majority or will Reform UK be the third party he has led that does better in social and electronic media than in seats in the House of Commons?

Experiencing history as it rolls forward has three advantages. First, it makes one aware that politicians and voters take decisions in conditions of high uncertainty with unforeseen as well as expected consequences that are often irreversible. Secondly, it has made me forward-looking, whereas concentrating on the latest news is backward-looking since the 24/7 flow of news quickly outdates this morning's news. This book is dynamic: the first part examines how the party system politicians are accustomed to was disrupted by the 2024 election; the second part concentrates on how individual parties are trying to mobilise popular support in this Parliament; and the conclusion sets out nine scenarios of possible outcomes of the next general election.

Between elections I have written many book comparing parties and elections on three continents and examining the problems of party government in Westminster, Washington and beyond. Like this book, they use ideas to give meaning to electoral data and use electoral data to distinguish between ideas that are interesting but improbable and those that are relevant to the British party system as it stands today. I write a monthly commentary for Electoral Calculus on what polls and predictions of seats mean for parties competing for control of government.

In fairness to readers who are curious to know how I vote, the answer is: I can't, because I am an American citizen. My preferred party, that of Harry Truman and Lyndon Johnson, does not contest British elections and, for that matter, no longer exists in the United States. My political outlook is perhaps best signified by a 60-year membership of the Reform Club in Pall Mall, where one can view issues, personalities and parties close to but independent of Westminster and Whitehall.

Professor Richard Rose
25 January 2026

Introduction: What British elections are about

A general election gives Britons three choices: people can vote for the candidate they want to represent their constituency in Parliament; the party that best represents their political views; or the party they want to form the government. However, individuals have only one vote. In an ideal world, one vote could achieve all three purposes. A voter's preferred candidate is nominated by the party they like and that party wins a parliamentary majority giving it control of government. Even if the party loses at a subsequent election, it will sooner or later regain control of government. The rotation of parties in office gives the great majority of voters the government of their choice some but not all of the time. This idealised system of British politics has ceased to exist.

The 2024 general election disrupted how elections work because it broke the link between parties winning votes, seats and control of government. An assortment of non-governing parties collectively won the biggest share of the popular vote, but their influence at Westminster has been diluted by fragmentation between

Liberal Democrats, the Greens, Scottish and Welsh nationalists and Reform UK MPs. The Labour government won only one-third of the national vote and the official Opposition, the Conservative Party, won less than one-quarter of the vote.

General elections are no longer general; the same two parties are not the main competitors in a majority of the 650 constituencies that collectively form the House of Commons designed for a governing party and an opposition. Instead, there are more than a dozen different combinations of parties finishing first and second. Labour and Conservative candidates came first and second in fewer than half of all constituencies. Reform UK is the major challenger to Labour MPs in the North of England and the Liberal Democrats are the main opposition to the Conservatives in the South of England.

This book is forward-looking: its aim is to explain how the disruption in the last general election will influence the outcome of the next election. Disruption has created a hybrid system in which more than half a dozen parties compete for votes and three parties compete for control of British government. Six parties have shown that they can compete for votes nationwide.

The book also takes into account unprecedented developments in the current Parliament. The Labour government and Keir Starmer personally have experienced an unprecedented early and deep slump in support. Reform UK, which won only five seats at the last election, has been coming first in opinion polls, making it a potential governing party. However, competition between three parties – Labour, the Conservatives and

Reform – creates the possibility that no party will win enough MPs to take control of government. While it is premature to predict the outcome of the next election, it is unwise to rely on past precedents to understand what current developments signify for the near future.

Since election results are decided nationwide, this book looks beyond studies that concentrate on the personalities and politics of Westminster. It examines the collective behaviour of tens of millions of ordinary people whose votes determine who represents them in the Westminster village. It goes beyond analyses of voter surveys by analysing what happens to the ballots that survey respondents cast. They are counted in 650 constituencies and the first-past-the-post system translates constituency results into a House of Commons of 650 MPs, the basis on which party leaders then form a government.

To understand the changes taking place in the British party system, this book is divided into three parts. The first part shows how the two-party system that developed after 1945 became a three-party system for half a century until its great disruption in the 2024 election. The second part shows where we are now, as the Labour government faces novel challenges outside the House of Commons from Reform UK and inside it from backbench Labour MPs. It also deals with a proliferation of fourth-force parties – the Liberal Democrats, Greens, nationalists and potentially parties formed of ex-Labour and Muslim MPs. The concluding part sets out alternative outcomes of the 2029 election. Outcomes range from a restoration of a majority government under Labour or Conservative leadership; a minority or coalition government; to a Parliament so divided that no government could be formed and a second election held that could institutionalise a new party system.

Where we've been

A two-party system prevailed between the 1950 and 1970 elections. The Liberal Party failed to establish itself as a governing party, winning only nine MPs in the 1950 election. The following year it contested only one-sixth of constituencies, taking only 2.6 per cent of the national vote. The Conservative and Labour Parties alternated in government and there was a close linkage between the voters' choice of their MP, party votes and control of government. Under six different prime ministers, the Conservative and Labour Parties together won an average of 93 per cent of the popular vote and 99 per cent of seats in the House of Commons.

The confrontation between the Tory government of Edward Heath and the trade unions in the two 'Who governs?' elections of 1974 resulted in a hybrid three-party system. The Liberals took advantage of the unpopularity of the two governing parties by nominating candidates in almost every constituency and winning nearly 20 per cent of the national vote. Concurrently, nationalist parties became credible competitors in Scotland, Wales and Northern Ireland. This resulted in the two governing parties winning between 67 per cent and 75 per cent of the total vote. In Parliaments returned in 1974, 2010 and 2017, the party winning the most seats fell just short of gaining an absolute parliamentary majority. These were incidents in a dynamic equilibrium in which the Labour and Conservative Parties showed their resilience by winning a parliamentary majority at the next election.

Since all three parties favoured British membership of the European Union, opponents of EU membership switched from a strategy of seeking votes and seats to a demand for a national referendum in which no party name would appear on the ballot. Thus, Conservative and Labour voters who did not like the EU could and did vote for leaving the EU without jeopardising their party's control of government. An absolute majority of the vote favoured Brexit in the 2016 referendum, more than four times the vote cast for the United Kingdom Independence Party at the 2015 general election. When the next 2019 election reverted to being a choice about government, voters returned to voting along party lines. The Conservative and Labour Parties together took 82 per cent of the vote, their highest share since 1970.

The 2024 general election disrupted the three-party system. Collectively, parties with no chance of leading a government won the largest share of the popular vote. The limited support for Labour, combined with a fall in the Conservative vote to a historic low, drove the two-party share of the vote down to 57 per cent. More than five-sixths of MPs represent fewer than half the voters in their constituency. Non-governing parties won 118 seats in total. Reform UK surpassed the Liberal Democrats in the popular vote, but because its support was relatively evenly spread it won only five seats. By concentrating campaigning in target seats for the first time in more than a century, the Liberal Democrats won 72 seats.

Instead of the Labour government being challenged in every constituency by the same party, the Tories are now the chief challengers in barely half the seats with Labour MPs. The Reform Party is in second place in 89 Labour seats, and the Scottish National Party is second in all the seats that Labour holds in Scotland. This is a sharp contrast with the 2017 election, when the Conservative and Labour candidates were in first and second place in 89 per cent of constituencies.

Voters now face a series of meta-choices that transcend the simple choice of candidate, party and government with a single ballot mark. First of all, there is a decision about voting for or against the government of the day. If the government is favoured, this is a simple choice. But if a voter's aim is to eject the governing party from office, they have up to half a dozen choices on their constituency ballot rather than the single alternative in the two-party system. The alternatives can be reduced by preferring parties with a similar ideology. But this still leaves the need to choose between one of three parties on the left or two parties on the right. Moreover, if their first choice of party has little hope of winning in their constituency, a voter must also decide whether to vote tactically. This involves a choice between wasting a vote's impact by favouring a party that represents their views but is very unlikely to win in their constituency or favouring a party with a chance to win the seat, whether it is positively viewed or seen as the lesser evil.

Where we are now

The fragmentation of competition into multiple dimensions challenges both voters and parties. The choice of parties is no longer confined to the one-dimensional left–right alternative. Voters now have a chance to vote for a constituency candidate who stands for green, anti-immigrant or national values, or for the mix offered by the 'fix the potholes' Liberal Democrats. However, this creates tension when the party that best represents a voter's political values is an also-ran in their constituency. Whether parties are locally competitive varies greatly between constituencies.

By becoming the government, Labour has lost the advantage of winning support as the only alternative to a failing Conservative government. It now offers voters the choice of voting for or against its own performance in government and voters have responded by bringing forward by two years the conventional mid-term slump in government support. The Starmer government started making unpopular policy choices within weeks of taking office and within nine months was making U-turns and trailing Reform UK in the opinion polls. Downing Street sought to stifle briefings by backbench Labour MPs and unnamed Cabinet ministers by publicly declaring that Keir Starmer would fight to remain party leader until the next general election. After a shambolic November 2025 budget, Labour MPs are discussing who will replace Starmer in the near future.

Even though it is the official opposition party in the House of Commons, the Conservative Party has so far failed to benefit from the electoral pendulum swinging away from the government. After losing almost half its vote at the last general election, it has now dropped an additional fifth in opinion polls. The chief reason why the Tories have narrowed the gap with Labour is that Labour's poll support has dropped even more. Kemi Badenoch has urged her party to be patient whilst she seeks to choose between the horns of a dilemma: to regain supporters lost to Reform UK by espousing a tough immigration policy or to seek defectors from the centre-left by offering a more moderate alternative than Reform to replace the Labour government. An appeal can be made to disaffected voters on both the right and left, but doing so risks falling between two stools.

Nigel Farage is demonstrating his charismatic capacity to disrupt the British party system. In the 2024 election Reform UK highlighted immigration, which both governing parties had not controlled and sought to avoid. It took third place in votes nationally and 95 per cent of its candidates saved their constituency deposits. However, it was a victim of the first-past-the-post electoral system, as its 14.3 per cent share of the popular vote won it less than 1 per cent of MPs. Labour's slump has reversed this bias. Since February 2025 Reform has been first in opinion polls with less than one-third of voter support; this is sufficient to give it upwards of half the seats in the House of Commons. In an effort to show that Reform UK is not just a one-man band, Farage has sought to institutionalise his charisma by creating a fully fledged party organisation with a quarter-million members and nationwide branches ready to fight local government, Scottish and Welsh elections and the next general election when it comes.

The breakthrough of Reform UK in the opinion polls has not only created three-way party competition to take control of government but also spawned a heterogeneous category of fourth-force parties. These are parties that have no chance or even do not want to control British government. It includes the Liberal Democrats, the Green Party and nationalist parties in Scotland, Wales and Northern Ireland. Collectively, fourth-force parties have more than one hundred MPs in the current Parliament and their combined support in opinion polls has become greater than that of either the Labour or Conservative Parties.

The Liberal Democrats and Green Party could have the biggest impact because they contest seats throughout Great Britain. If the Conservatives lose dozens of seats to Reform UK at the next election as current poll ratings suggest, the Liberal Democrats could even become a larger party than the Conservatives for the first time since 1910. However, this would not make the Liberal Democrats a potential governing party.

The Greens, initially a single-issue party focused on the environment, have gradually become a party with a full range of policies. At the 2024 election the Greens had their best result to date, gaining four MPs, and more than doubling their vote to 6.7 per cent, and for the first time a majority of their candidates saved their deposits. Zack Polanski, elected Green Party leader in September 2025 on a left-wing platform of eco-populism, has capitalised on Labour's loss of support. The party's poll support has doubled from that at the last election, but there are a limited number of constituencies where support is high enough to offer the chance of winning it. Since the Greens' rise in the polls takes voters from Labour, they could cost the governing party dozens of seats at the next election.

Among nationalist parties, the Scottish National Party can have the biggest impact on Westminster because Scotland returns 57 MPs. When Labour was doing well in 2024, the SNP won only nine seats. The fall in Labour support throughout Britain now favours the SNP taking dozens of Scottish seats from Labour. Wales has 32 Westminster MPs; the nationalist Plaid Cymru party won four of these seats in 2024. Since then polls indicate that Reform UK shared with Plaid Cymru the benefit in the fall in Labour's support. Northern Ireland parties differ in whether they favour a united Ireland governed from Dublin or union with Great Britain. Since its 18 seats were divided among six different parties in the 2024 election and Irish republicans do not take their seats at Westminster, Northern Ireland parties rarely have influence on votes in the House of Commons.

The influence of fourth-force parties depends on whether a single party wins an absolute majority in the House of Commons. This has usually been the case since 1950. The disruption of party competition at the 2024 election has left Reform UK and fourth-force parties well placed to compete for seats in more than three hundred constituencies. This increases the possibility of neither the two traditional governing parties nor

Reform winning a parliamentary majority at the next general election.

The resilience of the two governing parties will be severely tested at the next general election. Labour demonstrated resilience in the previous Parliament by backing off the left-wing appeal of Jeremy Corbyn, thus benefiting from the great fall in electoral support for the Conservative government. This time is different: there is now a massive swing against the performance of the Labour government. The Conservatives have survived for generations by recovering from losing control of government, but usually it has taken more than one general election to do so. Moreover, this time is doubly different. To win a parliamentary majority the Conservatives need to win two-hundred-plus seats in competition with Reform UK as well as Labour.

Where will we be at the next election?

Lots can happen between now and summer 2029, the latest date for holding the next general election. Nonetheless, as chapters 5 to 8 show, since July 2024 a lot has already happened that will affect the next election. In the minds of voters Labour has joined the Conservatives as being incompetent and distrusted in governing, and polls are showing that Reform UK has joined the two traditional governing parties in the competition to form the next British government. There are also known unknowns of electoral importance. For example, the Labour and Conservative party rules for calling a vote to change the party leader are known. Whether and when this will happen is unknown. The fact that the sword of Damocles hasn't fallen at the time of writing doesn't mean it is not there.

During a parliament there are three sources of fresh evidence about multi-dimensional party competition. By-elections produce real but unrepresentative evidence of the standing of the parties, because each contest involves only one-650th of the British electorate. Their occurrence is largely outside the control of government, usually occurring after the death of an MP or when an incumbent resigns because of involvement in financial or sexual misdoings. Because a by-election is not about the choice of government, voters can use their ballot to send a protest message to an unpopular government. Since Labour won more than four-fifths of its seats with less than half the vote, in many constituencies a Labour candidate is vulnerable to defeat if protest voters combine tactically to oust a Labour MP.

Opinion polls provide representative but unreal evidence, because respondents are asked which party they would vote for if an election were held now. However, the worse the standing of Labour in the polls, the stronger the incentive for the Labour government to delay facing the electorate until it is forced to do so. Random fluctuations in party support inherent in the sampling procedures used in polls mean that each party's support will appear to go up and down even when there is actually no change in their support. Furthermore, since opinion polls measure national trends in party support, they cannot be directly applied to the outcome of the 650 constituencies that elect MPs.

Given an electoral system that favours disproportional representation, multi-level regression and post-stratification (MRP) analysis can be used to predict the result in each of 650 constituencies and thus the number of MPs each party may win. To do this it combines survey data about the party preferences of different social groups with census data showing the size of each group in each constituency and its recent electoral history. The sum of these predictions shows the number of MPs each party would gain if an election were held today. MRP analysis is particularly useful to deal with Britain's multi-dimensional party system today, since it takes into account how party competition differs between constituencies. This far from a general election, MRP analyses provide evidence that the disruption of the party system is ongoing. Reform UK has leaped into first place in winning seats while the two governing parties and two fourth-force parties cluster close to each other in poll support.

Even though the result of a general election cannot be known in advance, it is possible to identify the various ways in which seats divided among parties can be combined in order to form a government. The scenarios vary in the degree to which they are precedented or unprecedented. One possible outcome is one of the two governing parties party winning a parliamentary majority and another is that a governing party forms a minority government on its own. There are at least three types of coalition government that parties active in the three-party system could form. Disruption can be maintained by any one of five different possible outcomes: a single-party Reform UK government; a coalition of two parties – Labour, Conservative or Reform; or parties so divided politically that no coalition could be formed and a second election must be called within weeks or a few months. As the title of the final chapter makes clear, the odds differ substantially on which scenario will match the outcome of the next general election.

Since 1945 a single party has formed a government with an *absolute parliamentary majority* after all but three of 22 general elections. This has not been the choice of voters, but a consequence of the first-past-the-post electoral system manufacturing a majority of seats from the winning party's minority of votes. Labour's massive 2024 majority shows that this can be done with as little as one-third of the national vote. It is currently unusual for any party to get 33 per cent support in the polls. When support for the leading party falls below 30 per cent, as has been the case in the monthly average of polls since October 2024, the likelihood of any party winning an absolute majority of seats falls sharply.

A *single-party minority government* can be formed if the leading party is only a limited number of seats short of a majority. This happened in 2017 when the Conservative government fell nine seats short of an absolute majority and entered into a transactional relationship with the Democratic Unionist Party. Nationalist fourth-force parties would be easiest to accommodate since they would want increased devolved powers to the Scottish Parliament or the Welsh Senedd rather than seats in a British Parliament.

A *coalition government* offers a party with a plurality but not a majority of seats the opportunity to occupy Downing Street if it shares Cabinet posts with a party whose MPs create a coalition majority. When the Conservative Party fell 20 seats short of a majority in 2010, David Cameron formed a coalition with the Liberal Democrats in which the Liberal leader, Nick Clegg, was deputy prime minister. Since Labour, the Liberal Democrats and the Green Party all have left-of-centre views on policy, there is a policy basis for a coalition government. However, there are electoral grounds for the Liberal Democrats and Greens rejecting such a coalition. It would mean tying themselves to serve under a Labour prime minister whose party had lost more than one hundred seats, thereby creating its need for a coalition.

If Labour, the Conservatives and Reform UK each had upwards of 175 seats, three different coalitions would be arithmetically possible, but face major political obstacles. A Labour–Reform coalition would be a non-starter on political grounds. A Reform–Conservative coalition would have limited differences on policy but a fundamental difference about which party swallowed the other. Farage's aim is to replace the Conservative Party, not to prop it up in government. A Labour–Conservative coalition government could be justified if their leaders believed that keeping Reform UK out of office was a price worth paying for joining together – and that such a cartel would not create a backlash benefiting Reform.

If no combination of parties was able to agree on the formation of a new government, then by default Labour would remain a caretaker government until a second election could be held a few months later. A second election could end ongoing disruption by restoring the three-party system or a coalition government. However, a second election could produce the same divisions as before. If that were the case, it would be a gamble to call a third election in hopes the electorate would 'get it right', that is, produce a parliamentary majority for a stable government. An alternative would be to accept the electorate's repeated disruption of the established party system and create a new party system.

While many scenarios exist, only one scenario can fit what happens. The majority will become might-have-been scenarios. The list of different scenarios leaves open the odds on each alternative. If the odds on each were equal, then there would be barely a one-in-ten chance of the result being a majority government. A more realistic assumption is that the odds on different outcomes are not equal.

As you don't need a PhD to be interested in who governs Britain, this book is written in language free of technical jargon and copious citations more appropriate to an academic article. Readers who are interested in political theory will know which concepts I have drawn upon in writing this book. Readers who want to rummage around election statistics can find a plenitude of data in sources listed in the Appendix. Opinion-poll data and MRP results can be updated by accessing online links listed there.

Part I

Where we've been

1

Two stable British party systems

The theory of the British two-party system postulates competition for control of government between two parties. Although a third party can make it impossible for the two governing parties to claim 100 per cent of the vote, the first-past-the-post electoral system excludes it from government by converting the plurality vote of the leading party into a parliamentary majority. Notwithstanding the familiarity of the two-party system, it has not characterised British party politics for more than half a century.

In practice British parties have competed for control of government in six different systems since the first steps were taken towards democratic elections in the nineteenth century. Each was created by the disruption of the preceding system through major changes in electoral law and/or the emergence of new parties winning sufficient votes and seats to influence control of government. The new system then maintained an equilibrium for decades, as votes, seats and control of government fluctuated between the same set of parties. Up to a point, the system showed its resilience when challenged by a minority or coalition government. However, sooner or later the system was abruptly disrupted by the shortcomings of the governing parties and a new party system emerged.

The rationalisation though not the democratisation of the right to vote in the 1832 Reform Act was followed by the first party system reflecting election results, a two-party system of competition between the newly founded Liberal and Conservative Parties. Party organisations recruiting mass memberships at the constituency level were created by the Conservatives under Benjamin Disraeli and the Liberals under William Gladstone.

The 1885 election introduced a four-party system in which Irish nationalists and a breakaway Liberal Unionist Party were able to win sufficient seats to influence control of government rotating between parties for and against Irish home rule. The Labour Representation Committee began nominating candidates in 1900 and winning dozens of seats. The First World War was fought under a three-party coalition government of Liberal, Conservative and Labour MPs. The general election of December 1918 was disruptive. A coalition of Conservative and Liberal MPs led by David Lloyd George defeated anti-coalition Liberals and Conservative candidates, and the Labour Party nominated candidates in a majority of British constituencies. Irish nationalists were replaced by Sinn Fein, which led to the creation of the Irish Free State and the removal of Irish nationalist influence on control of British government.

In the third system, which prevailed from 1922 to 1945, control of government alternated between being in the hands of a majority party, a minority party or a three-party coalition. In 1922 and 1924 the Conservative Party under Stanley Baldwin formed majority governments; Labour and the Liberals were in opposition. The Labour Party formed minority governments after the 1923 and 1929 elections. During the 1931 economic crisis a National government was formed dependent on Conservative MPs but with ex-Labour leader J. Ramsay MacDonald as prime minister and National Liberal ministers. It was re-elected in 1935. When the Second World War showed the failure of that government's appeasement policy, Winston Churchill became the head of a three-party coalition with Labour leader Clement Attlee serving as deputy prime minister and independent Liberals were also ministers. The 1945 general election disrupted the interwar three-party system. The Labour Party won a big parliamentary majority in competition with Churchill's attempt to keep alive a Conservative-led national coalition.

The fourth system, which resulted from the 1950 general election, was once again a two-party system but with a change of parties. The Conservative and Labour Parties virtually monopolised the vote and the Liberal Party became irrelevant. The fifth party system was a hybrid created by the two 1974 elections when the Liberal Party took advantage of the unpopularity of the two governing parties to win almost one-fifth of the national vote. This created a three-party system of electoral competition. However, it was a hybrid, since the first-past-the-post electoral system usually kept the renamed Liberal Democrats' share of MPs so low that control of government remained in the hands of the Labour and Conservative Parties.

This chapter shows how the two-party and hybrid three-party systems maintained their stability for almost three-quarters of a century. The hybrid change kept control of government the same but seriously affected competition for votes. Occasional challenges showed the resilience of the hybrid system. This chapter focuses on the two systems that still shape many expectations of how Britons choose a government. Subsequent chapters show how these expectations have been eroded by changes in parties and in the electorate, resulting in the disruption of the 2024 election and what has followed.

The classic two-party system, 1950–70

In a stable party system, only the names of the parties competing for control of government are fixed. Democratic theory stipulates that the votes of competing parties should go up and down enough so that control of government can rotate between them. Whatever the volatility of the vote between successive elections, stability is maintained if there is no change in the parties rotating in and out of government or a substantial trend down in the governing parties' votes and seats. If the long-term effects of these fluctuations tend to cancel each other out, the party system is in a stable equilibrium. This was the case in the British party system for two decades from 1950.

Fluctuations without systemic change

The 1950 general election introduced a two-party system instead of the three-party system that had been in place between the two world wars. The Labour government of Clement Attlee won a parliamentary majority. Together the Labour and Conservative Parties won 98.1 per cent of the seats in the House of Commons and 89.5 per cent of the United Kingdom vote (Table 1.1). The Liberal Party tried and failed to remain a relevant third party. More than two-thirds of its 475 candidates lost their deposits because they did not gain as much as one-eighth of their constituency's vote. The Liberals gained only nine MPs, which was then the party's worst showing in its history.

The 1951 election institutionalised two-party competition for seats at the constituency level. Labour and Conservative candidates were the only names on the ballot in four-fifths of all constituencies. The Liberals nominated candidates in fewer than one-sixth of seats, and there were only 33 independent or nationalist candidates. Thus, the two parties' combined share of the national vote reached a record high of 96.8 per cent, and together they won 98.6 per cent of all seats. Although Labour came first in the national vote, it did not come first where it counted. The Conservatives came first in a majority of 630 constituencies, and Winston Churchill became prime minister.

Control of government rotated three times in two decades, while the government of the day was re-elected

Table 1.1 The classic two-party system 1950–70

	Seats fought N	Vote %	MPs N	MPs %
1950				
Labour	617	46.1	315	50.4
Conservative	619	43.4	298	47.7
Two-party share (%)	66.1	89.5	613	98.1
1951				
Conservative	617	48.0	321	51.4
Labour	617	48.8	295	47.2
Two-party share (%)	89.7	96.8	616	98.6
1955				
Conservative	624	49.7	345	54.7
Labour	620	46.4	277	44.0
Two-party share (%)	88.3	96.1	622	98.7
1959				
Conservative	625	46.6	365	57.9
Labour	621	43.8	258	41.0
Two-party share (%)	81.1	90.4	623	98.9
1964				
Labour	628	44.1	317	50.3
Conservative	630	43.4	304	48.2
Two-party share (%)	71.6	87.5	621	98.5
1966				
Labour	622	48.0	364	57.7
Conservative	620	41.3	253	40.1
Two-party share (%)	72.8	89.3	617	97.9
1970				
Conservative	628	46.4	330	52.4
Labour	625	43.1	288	45.7
Two-party share (%)	68.2	89.5	618	98.1

Source: Rallings and Thrasher (2012). There were 625 constituencies in 1950 and 1951 and 630 constituencies thereafter.

four times. In 1951 the Conservative Party took control of government in its own name for the first time since 1924. The Labour opposition was unable to oust the Conservative governments of Anthony Eden and Harold Macmillan until the 1964 election. After 13 years of Conservative rule Harold Wilson became prime minister campaigning with the slogan 'It's time for a change'. When Labour sought re-election to a third term in office in 1970, Wilson was replaced by a Conservative government led by Edward Heath.

There was little fluctuation in the votes and seats of the governing parties. Labour's high point in votes, 48.8 per cent of the national total, came in 1951; however, it lost control of government because the Conservative Party won a majority of MPs. Labour's low point in votes, 43.1 per cent, brought defeat in 1970. The change in Labour's vote from one election to the next averaged 2.4 percentage points. Its biggest change occurred in 1970, when its vote dropped by 4.9 percentage points. The smallest change was in 1964, when Labour's vote went up only 0.3 percentage points; it nonetheless won the election because the Conservative vote went down more. Labour averaged 45.7 per cent of the national vote in seven elections from 1950 to 1970.

The Conservative vote likewise fluctuated little. The party's vote share reached a peak of 49.7 per cent in 1955, the highest winning share at any postwar general election. Its lowest vote, 41.3 per cent, came in 1966, when the Labour government came close to its peak vote. The change in the Conservative vote from one election to the next averaged 2.7 percentage points. It changed least in 1955, when it rose 1.7 percentage points and most in 1951, when a rise of 4.6 points enabled the Conservatives to take control of government. Indicative of the even balance in the vote of the governing parties, the average Tory vote, 45.6 per cent, was virtually identical to that of Labour.

With only two parties competing for votes, the change in the national vote from one election to the next could be illustrated on television by the one-dimensional swing of a pendulum. When the percentage of votes for one party went up, the vote for the other party went down. Of crucial importance for the allocation of seats, the change in votes in hundreds of constituencies was much the same in size and almost always in the same direction as at the national level. Consistency in the movement of votes at the constituency level showed that general elections were general. Nationwide influences rather than local factors and candidates determined whether the outcome was a Conservative or a Labour government (Butler, 1955: 202f).

The first-past-the-post electoral system ensured that the outcome of seats in the House of Commons was disproportional: the governing party always received a bigger share of seats than of votes. The competition for seats often produced a wafer-thin majority for the winning party, because the Opposition also was high in votes and seats. In most elections in the period, the governing party's Commons majority was no higher than 13 seats above the minimum. In 1964 Harold Wilson had only one more MP than the minimum required for an absolute parliamentary majority. The Conservatives won a high of 365 seats in 1959, and seven years later Labour peaked with 364 seats. Both achievements were significantly below the high-water marks achieved under three-party competition by Margaret Thatcher and Tony Blair.

For two decades the distribution of votes and seats was stable. In 1950 the victorious Labour Party secured 46.1 per cent of the vote; in 1970 the winning Conservative Party took virtually the same share, 46.4 per cent (Table 1.1). After being ousted from Downing Street, each party showed its resilience by regaining control of government.

A hybrid three-party system, 1974–2019

The failure of Labour and Conservative efforts to achieve economic growth and control inflation between 1964 and 1974 resulted in the disruption of the classic two-party system. The two governing parties' share of the vote fell to 75 per cent in the February 1974 election. This was the lowest two-party total since 1929. The Liberals filled the gap. Their share of the vote rose from 7.5 to 19.3 per cent. However, the first-past-the-post electoral system gave the Liberals only 14 MPs.

The three-party system that emerged was a hybrid. Competition for votes between three parties became normal, as the renamed Liberal Democrats took a significant share of the national vote. This meant that at times the vote for both governing parties went down. However, in 13 elections the Conservative and Labour Parties maintained their duopoly control of Downing

Street. Even when the governing party lacked a majority of MPs, the influence of third parties was limited and transactional. The Liberal Democrats secured a referendum on changing the voting system, and the Scottish National Party (SNP) a referendum on independence. In both cases the parties promoting radical change in the system lost.

Fluctuations in votes, not seats

Thanks to the first-past-the-post electoral system, the two front-running parties dominated the House of Commons (Table 1.2). Their peak strength was in 1979, when together they won 608 of the 635 seats. The weakness of the Conservative opposition between 1997 and 2010 gave the Liberal Democrats the opportunity to win as many as 62 seats in 2005 without disturbing the Blair government's control of Parliament. This reduced the two governing parties to their lowest number of MPs in the period, 85 per cent of the Commons total. The Liberal Democrats' participation in a coalition with the Conservatives caused the Lib Dems to lose seven-eighths of their seats at the 2015 election. The SNP benefited from Labour's weakness in that election by winning 56 seats in Scotland. A byproduct of this gain was that it more than doubled the Conservative government's majority over Labour.

The vote of the governing parties fluctuated more in the three-party system than in the two-party system. This was because defecting Labour and Conservative voters now had two parties to choose from. They could

Table 1.2 The hybrid three-party system 1974–2019

Year	Con		Lab		Lib Dem	
	Votes (%)	Seats (N)	Votes (%)	Seats (N)	Votes (%)	Seats (N)
Feb. 1974	37.9	297	37.2	301	19.3	14
Oct. 1974	35.8	277	39.3	319	18.3	13
1979	43.9	339	36.9	269	13.8	11
1983	42.4	397	27.6	209	25.4	23
1987	42.3	376	30.8	229	22.6	22
1992	41.9	336	34.4	271	17.8	20
1997	30.7	165	43.2	418	16.8	46
2001	31.6	166	40.7	412	18.3	52
2005	32.4	198	35.2	355	22.0	62
2010	36.1	306	29.0	258	23.0	57
2015	36.8	330	30.4	232	7.9	8
2017	42.3	317	40.0	262	7.4	12
2019	43.6	365	32.1	202	11.5	12

Source: https://researchbriefings.files.parliament.uk/documents/CBP-7529/CBP-7529.pdf#page=8

vote for the centrist Liberal Democrats or for the alternative party of government. In Scotland and Wales nationalist parties offered defectors an additional choice. Moreover, fluctuations in the vote of the two governing parties were no longer symmetrical; both could go up or down together depending on the electoral appeal of the Liberal Democrats at a particular election.

The widening of choice resulted in the fluctuation in the vote of both governing parties, particularly Labour, showing more volatility than in the two-party system. The Labour Party's vote fluctuated an average of only 2.4 percentage points in two-party competition while fluctuating more than twice as much, 5.3 points, during three-party competition. By contrast, the fluctuation in the Conservative vote was steady. It fluctuated an average of 2.7 percentage points in two-party competition and 3.5 points in the three-party system.

The Conservative vote fell by one-fifth in February 1974, its biggest drop since 1945. However, it quickly recovered under the leadership of Margaret Thatcher, taking 43.9 per cent of the vote in 1979 and staying on this plateau for the next three elections. After 18 years in office, the Conservative vote fell to 30.7 per cent in 1997, then the lowest in the party's history. Its support remained below one-third in the next two elections. Small increases in the Conservative vote resulted in David Cameron becoming prime minister in 2010 thanks to the bigger drop in Labour support. In 2019 the vote for the 'Get Brexit done' party rose back to the level it had been at four decades earlier. Altogether, the Conservative vote went up seven times and down six times between 1974 and 2019.

After losing the 1979 election the Labour Party faced a threat to its existence from the Social Democratic Party (SDP), a breakaway led by four Labour ex-Cabinet ministers rejecting the leftward lurch of the Labour Party under Michael Foot. The SDP and the Liberals, with whom it shared many views, formed an Alliance to contest the 1983 election. Labour fought the election on a manifesto that was wryly described as the longest suicide note in history. The Alliance was defeated by the first-past-the-post electoral system. Its 25.4 per cent share of the popular vote won it only 23 MPs because its centrist vote was widespread. By contrast, Labour's 27.6 per cent of the vote won it 206 MPs, because its vote was heavily concentrated in traditional Labour strongholds. Thus, Labour lost its deposit in 119 seats while the Alliance lost only 11 deposits. At the 1987 election the Alliance won 22.6 per cent of the popular vote and 22 MPs. Failure to replace Labour as the alternative party of government led the SDP to merge with the Liberal Party, which was renamed the Liberal Democrats or Lib Dems for short.

After trailing more than 14 percentage points behind the Tories in 1983 the Labour Party became resilient under the leadership of Neil Kinnock, but it only got as far as almost halving the Conservative lead at the 1992 election. Tony Blair capitalised on the Conservative government's long tenure in office by leading what he called New Labour in a 'time for a change' election. Labour's 1997 vote went up almost 9 percentage points to 43.2 per cent and it won 418 MPs, a party record. The Blair-led government then won the next two elections with a falling vote, thanks to the Conservatives' difficulties in recovering in competition with the Liberal Democrats as well as with Labour. The economic crisis of 2008 dropped the Labour vote to 29.0 per cent in 2010, its lowest since 1918. It then went up and down substantially in the three elections in the next decade.

Three-party competition meant that the electoral pendulum no longer followed a fixed path between the Labour and Conservative Parties in which what one party gained in votes was matched by what the other party lost. Instead, the exchange of votes became more like a merry-go-round, as voters circulated between parties, getting on and off at different stops.

Relevant and irrelevant parties seeking votes

For a third party to be relevant in electoral competition it needs to nominate candidates to fight the great majority of the United Kingdom's constituencies; it needs to save its deposit in a substantial majority of the seats it fights; and it needs to contest general elections from one decade to the next.

The *Liberal Party* made its breakthrough as a relevant party by nominating 517 candidates nationwide in the February 1974 election. This was the most candidates the party had nominated since 1906. Even though candidates were standing in hundreds of seats that the party had not contested for decades, the average vote per candidate more than doubled. The Liberals saved 494 constituency deposits at a time when 12.5 per cent of a constituency's vote was needed to get the deposit refunded. At the preceding election in 1970, a majority of its candidates had lost their deposits. However, constituency support was widespread but not deep, making the Liberals a victim of the first-past-the-post electoral system. The party won only 14 seats. This made the three-party system a hybrid, since the Liberal Democrats won enough votes to reduce the governing parties' combined share of the vote to 75 per cent but lacked the seats to compete for control of government.

The Liberal Democrats' share of the national vote has fluctuated substantially in both absolute and relative terms, not only because of changes in party strategy but also in the amount of support coming from voters dissatisfied with one or both governing parties. The party's change in vote between elections averaged only 2.7 percentage points in the two-party system but was 4.9 per cent in the three-party system. The Liberal Democrat vote went up by more than 11 percentage points in February 1974, and the vote of both governing parties fell. This happened again when the Alliance vote almost doubled the Liberals' previous support. Its biggest drop, 15 percentage points in 2015, came when many supporters deserted the party in reaction to it spending five years as a junior partner in a Conservative-led coalition government. The number of seats it won only roughly correlated with its popular vote. The Liberal Democrats' 62 MPs were as irrelevant in the 2005 Parliament when Labour had an absolute majority of MPs as were its eight MPs facing a Conservative majority in the 2015 House of Commons.

Nationalist parties contest only the limited number of seats in their nation: 57 in Scotland, 32 in Wales and 18 in Northern Ireland. Thus, their share of the UK vote is irrelevant, but they almost invariably retain their deposits in Scotland and Wales. The SNP normally finishes first or second in votes in competition with Labour. However, its share of the Scottish vote in British elections fluctuates substantially. In 2015 the SNP won 50 per cent of the Scottish vote and all but three of Scotland's MPs. Its vote and seats then fell substantially at the election two years later only to have both rise again in 2019. The SNP's relevance to

British government depends not on how strong it is at Westminster but on how weak the governing parties are in the House of Commons.

Plaid Cymru's support has not been relevant in the UK Parliament because it is limited to Wales. It won its highest share of the vote, 14.3 per cent, in 2001, but that left it third in Welsh votes. Its lowest share of the vote was at the 2019 election, 9.9 per cent. Because Plaid Cymru's appeal is concentrated in Welsh-speaking regions, the number of seats it wins depends on what happens there; it won four seats when its vote was at its relative peak and held on to the same number when its vote was at its relative lowest. By contrast with its weakness at Westminster, Plaid Cymru is relevant in electoral competition in the devolved Welsh Senedd.

The *Northern Ireland party system* was half-integrated into the British party system until 1971. The Ulster Unionist Party, which won all or nearly all of Ulster's 12 Westminster seats, supported the Conservative Party. A variety of Irish nationalists and republicans expressed their opposition to British rule by refusing to take their seats at Westminster (Elliott, 1972). Following the suspension of the Northern Ireland Parliament in 1972, the Ulster Unionists broke from the British Conservatives. The Democratic Unionist Party led by Dr Ian Paisley replaced the Ulster Unionists, and Sinn Fein and the Social Democratic and Labour Party became the two Irish unity parties. With just 18 seats divided among up to six parties, only in unusual circumstances have Northern Ireland MPs been relevant to control of British government.

The *Green Party* began nominating candidates in 1987 but only began contesting a majority of constituencies in 2010, when it won its first MP. This encouraged it to nominate more candidates but it remained irrelevant in 2019, losing 93 per cent of its 497 deposits and winning only 2.7 per cent of the national vote. Its breakthrough into the ranks of relevant parties did not occur until 2024 (see chapter 8).

Throughout the period the British electorate demonstrated their distaste for far-right politics by not voting for fascist parties. The National Front Party, bearing the name of the prewar party of Hitler-apologist Sir Oswald Mosley, has contested 12 elections since 1970 and never won enough votes to save a constituency deposit. The British National Party has contested ten elections since 1983, when it nominated 54 candidates who won an average of 270 votes per constituency. The lowering of the standard for saving a deposit to 5 per cent before the 1987 election enabled the party to save three or more deposits at each of four subsequent elections. The British National Party's relatively best showing was in 2010, when it nominated 338 candidates and saved more than one-fifth of its deposits, gaining 1.9 per cent of the national vote. It then experienced internal quarrelling and nominated only one candidate in 2019.

Europe challenges both governing parties

All three parties in the hybrid party system supported British membership in the European Economic Community when it joined in 1973. However, there were divisions of opinion about membership in both the electorate and the parties. In 1975 Prime Minister Harold Wilson called a referendum on whether the UK should remain in Europe. Two-thirds voted in favour of remaining. However, the 32.8 per cent vote in favour of withdrawal was relevant by the standards of a general election (Butler and Kitzinger, 1976).

The increase in European integration in the 1992 Maastricht Treaty stimulated the formation of two single-issue anti-European Union parties to campaign for a referendum on the United Kingdom's membership in the EU. At the 1997 general election the *Referendum Party*, funded by Sir James Goldsmith, nominated candidates in 547 seats but won only 2.6 per cent of the vote, and 505 of its candidates lost their deposits. It was dissolved shortly after the election. Reflecting internal divisions within the anti-EU movement, at the same election the *United Kingdom Independence Party* (UKIP) contested 193 seats and won three-tenths of 1 per cent of the vote. The only candidate saving their deposit was Nigel Farage.

To advance the anti-EU cause, UKIP began pressing for a referendum on withdrawal from the EU, while also nominating hundreds of parliamentary candidates threatening to take votes from the governing parties (Ford and Goodwin, 2014). In 2001 all but six candidates lost their deposits. In the 2010 election, 99 of its 588 candidates saved their deposit and UKIP took 3.1 per cent of the national vote. As a pressure group targeting Conservative MPs as well as voters, UKIP got

David Cameron to pledge to call a referendum if the Conservatives won the 2015 general election. They did, with UKIP taking 12.6 per cent of the national vote but gaining only one seat.

Since House of Commons seats were not at stake in the 2016 European Union referendum, cross-party groups formed to campaign for and against Brexit. There was a 51.9 per cent majority in favour of leaving the EU. David Cameron immediately resigned as prime minister and was succeeded by Theresa May. She called a snap election in 2017, expecting to win an increased majority, but instead won only a plurality of MPs and formed a minority government. This was followed by two years of debates on the terms of Brexit, in which cross-party votes of MPs rejected 15 different measures as the date for leaving the EU rapidly approached (Rose, 2020: chapter 11).

A pair of elections in 2019 showed how the electorate voted very differently depending on the issue at hand. When an election to the European Parliament was held in 2019, the UK participated because it had not yet left the EU. Control of government was not at stake; votes were cast for parties depending on the clarity of their position for or against the EU. The anti-EU Brexit Party led by Nigel Farage came first with 32 per cent of the vote and the strongly pro-EU Liberal Democrats came second with 20 per cent of the vote. Labour finished third with 14 per cent of the vote and the Conservatives came fifth with 9 per cent. Theresa May resigned as prime minister and was succeeded by Boris Johnson.

The December 2019 election to decide control of British government marked a return to hybrid three-party competition (cf. McAllister and Rose, 2020; Curtice, 2020). When voters were asked to choose who governs Britain rather than who they wanted to represent them in the European Parliament, the Conservative Party won majority control of government with its biggest share of the popular vote since Margaret Thatcher's 1979 victory. Even though Labour was led by the massively unpopular Jeremy Corbyn, it won almost a million more votes than at the 2015 election. Together, the two governing parties won 75 per cent of the total vote. The combined vote for the two opposing parties putting the EU issue foremost – the Liberal Democrats and the Brexit Party – was 14 per cent.

A resilient equilibrium

A party system in equilibrium needs a balance between stability and change. To keep control of government, the governing party must be resilient in responding to fresh challenges. This is in keeping with the principle that the Conservative Lord David Cecil set out in 1912: 'Even when I changed, it was to conserve.' Stability in a democratic system also requires that control of government changes hands from time to time. For this to occur, an opposition party must also be resilient, learning to understand why it lost control of government and regaining enough votes to get back into government.

The extent of change in the party system as a whole is shown by the total volatility in the vote of all parties.

In a two-party system, an increase in the percentage of one party's vote is complemented by the other party's loss. In a system with three or more parties, a single party's gains or losses are likely to be divided among several parties. In the classic two-party system, the combined fluctuation in the vote for the Conservative and Labour Parties from one election to the next averaged only 6.0 per cent. The disruption of this system in February 1974 produced a 14.4 percentage point fall in the combined vote of the two governing parties and a double-digit boost in the Liberal vote. Volatility then went up and down at a higher level in keeping with political events. The SDP intervention in 1983 pushed volatility up to 22 per cent, and Labour's ousting of the Conservatives in 1997 brought it to 21 per cent. Volatility reached a peak of 26.7 per cent in 2015 as the Liberal Democrat vote collapsed and UKIP gained double-digit support, while the vote of each of the two governing parties was virtually unchanged.

Rotation in control of government

The rotation of parties in and out of government involves a process in which the governing party's forced and unforced errors become more important to voters than the attractive features that won it control of government. It also depends on the tempo at which the opposition party, after one or more election defeats, adopts a strategy that will win the votes it needs to regain office.

Because the governing party holds office by winning a parliamentary majority, it can lose seats at an election and still retain control of government. It can continue indefinitely thanks to the advantages of office until unexpected or unwanted events cause its support to crash. The official opposition faces multiple handicaps to regaining office. It carries into a new parliament responsibility for unpopular measures that led to its electoral defeat and it can take years for a party's faults in government to fade from the minds of voters. The diagnosis of the reasons for defeat can open up divisions within the opposition about who is to blame for the defeat, what should be done to regain support, and who is best able to lead the party to victory. Until it can unite around a policy and a leader that attract fresh electoral support, it must wait for the governing party's support to erode gradually or crash.

During the hybrid period of three-party competition, control of government changed five times. After five years of struggling with economic management, the Labour government under Jim Callaghan lost the 1979 election to the Conservative Party under Margaret Thatcher. With the help of a divided opposition, Thatcher led the party to re-election twice and her successor, John Major, led the Conservatives to a fourth straight victory in 1992 with a vote that was only 2 percentage points less than Thatcher had initially won. Five months after winning re-election the Major government crashed when there was a dramatic run on the pound that remained in the minds of the electorate when they cast their votes at the next election, which resulted in government rotating into Labour's hands.

The Labour government of Tony Blair entered office with a comfortable 12.5-percentage-point lead over the Conservatives. Its support gradually contracted to 35.2 per cent in 2005, at that time the lowest share of the vote for any majority government since the introduction of democratic elections. Nonetheless, given the slowness of the Conservative opposition to recover, Blair's government twice won re-election. By the time Tony Blair announced his retirement in 2007 Labour had fallen significantly behind the Conservatives in the polls. Thus, the economic crash that hit his successor Gordon Brown added to the size of Labour's defeat after 13 years in government.

After rotating into office in 2010 the Conservative government's career has been atypical: its vote increased rather than declined and the party won re-election three times. This was because David Cameron became prime minister in 2010 with a share of the vote so low that it fell 20 seats short of gaining a parliamentary majority. The quirks of three-party competition and the first-past-the-post electoral system meant that the Conservatives won a majority of 330 seats in 2015, even though its vote went up less than 1 percentage point. Even though the party's vote went up by 5.5 percentage points in 2017, it fell nine seats short of a majority and Theresa May led an unstable minority government. Normality was restored in 2019 when Boris Johnson led the Conservative Party to its fourth successive election victory in 2019 with a share of the vote that was the highest of any government in forty years.

Resilience keeps government in two pairs of hands

Election outcomes three times challenged the governing party remaining in office during a parliament because it lacked a parliamentary majority. Each time the situation was resolved by the resilience of the governing party: it won an absolute majority of seats in the election that followed.

When Labour fell 17 seats short of an absolute majority in the February 1974 election, Prime Minister Harold Wilson showed resilience. To hold off the Scottish Nationalist challenge to Labour seats, he promised to introduce devolution. In the October election that followed, even though the SNP gained both votes and seats, Labour won a majority thanks to Conservatives losing both votes and seats. After Labour lost its very slim majority in the new Parliament due to by-election defeats and defections, a deal with the Liberals and the SNP on devolution enabled Labour to continue as a minority government for almost its full five-year term until referendums in Scotland and Wales rejected devolution. Opposition parties large and small then combined to bring down the Labour government by a vote of no confidence.

The Conservatives won the most seats in the 2010 election but fell short of an absolute majority. To get into Downing Street after 13 years in opposition, David Cameron made a coalition government with the Liberal Democrats acting as a junior partner, the first peacetime coalition since 1931. The agreement specified holding a referendum about changing the electoral system to one more favourable to the Lib Dems. It also specified that the Conservatives could campaign against changing the electoral system, which they did in company with Labour. The upshot was that a change putting the two parties at risk of losing their duopolistic control of government was rejected by 67 per cent of voters. At the next general election Cameron won a majority for the Conservatives governing on their own.

Theresa May called a snap general election in spring 2017 in the expectation of increasing her authority by winning a parliamentary majority in her own right. Instead, the election left the Conservatives nine seats short of an absolute majority. May's government became dependent for a majority on a transactional arrangement concerning the special interests of Northern Ireland's Democratic Unionist Party. She resigned in spring 2019 after failing to secure a parliamentary majority on terms for withdrawing from the European Union. The party system regained its equilibrium in 2019 when Boris Johnson led the Conservatives to their biggest parliamentary majority since 1983.

Both governing parties have shown resilience in dealing with the Scottish National Party and Plaid Cymru by devolving to the Scottish Parliament and the Welsh Senedd powers that they do not like to bother with in London, such as looking after local government, while keeping powers they value in Whitehall. Invoking the principle of equal representation among all nations of the UK, Tony Blair's Labour government cut Scotland's representation in the Westminster parliament from 72 seats to 59. In response to demands of the

SNP-led Scottish government for more tax revenue, the Treasury backed the devolution of tax-raising powers to Scotland, so that the Edinburgh Parliament rather than Westminster could be blamed for tax increases. The one power that has not been devolved is that of calling a referendum on independence. Thus, SNP demands for a referendum on independence can be rejected out of hand at Westminster.

Both governing parties have sought to protect themselves against additional parties breaking into the hybrid three-party system by taking over their policies, a practice going back to the 1860s strategy of the Conservatives stealing the Liberal policy of expanding the franchise. The Labour Party has sought to avoid losing votes to the Green Party by adopting net zero policies, and the Conservatives took over Brexit from Nigel Farage's UKIP party and are now seeking to take immigration policies from Farage's Reform UK party.

Conservative governments have shown resilience by five prime ministers resigning in the middle of a parliament when opinion polls and by-elections showed they had become an electoral liability. Harold Macmillan used a short stay in hospital as the rationale for resigning in 1963. When Conservative MPs forced a vote on Margaret Thatcher remaining prime minister in 1990, after falling just short of winning the super-majority needed to remain in office, she resigned rather than lead a divided party. David Cameron resigned after a referendum vote endorsed Brexit, and Theresa May resigned after the disastrous Conservative showing in the 2019 European Parliament election. Boris Johnson left in 2022 after cabinet ministers resigned. No Labour prime minister has yet been forced from office by their own MPs.

The core vote of the two governing parties remained in equilibrium from 1974 to 2019. In February 1974 Labour and the Conservatives had a combined vote of 75.1 per cent. Forty-five years later their combined vote was 75.7 per cent. However, the people casting their votes were slowly but steadily changing. A majority of voters in 2019 had not been born when the 1970 election was held and there has also been almost a complete demographic turnover in the electorate between 1950 and 2019. Even more important, the attachment to parties a century or two old has weakened greatly. The political outlook of 21st-century voters cannot be reduced to a simple choice between two parties.

Citations

Butler, David, 1955. *The British General Election of 1955*. London: Macmillan.

Butler, David and Kitzinger, Uwe, 1976. *The 1975 Referendum*. London: Macmillan.

Curtice, John, 2020. 'A return to "normality" at last: how the electoral system worked in 2019'. In J. Tonge, S. Wilks-Heeg and L. Thompson, eds, *Britain Votes: The 2019 General Election*. Oxford: Oxford University Press.

Elliott, Sydney, 1972. *Northern Ireland Parliamentary Election Results, 1921–72*. Chichester: Political Reference Publications.

Ford, Robert and Goodwin, Matthew, 2014. *Revolt on the Right: Explaining Support for the Radical Right in Britain*. Abingdon: Routledge.

McAllister, Ian and Rose, Richard, 2020. 'When institutions and issues change, voting changes'. In R. Rose, *How Referendums Challenge European Democracy*. London: Palgrave Macmillan.
Rallings, Colin and Thrasher, Michael, 2012. *British Electoral Facts, 1832–2012*. London: Biteback.
Rose, Richard, 2020. *How Referendums Challenge European Democracy*. London: Palgrave Macmillan.

2

Voters becoming detached from parties

Voters and parties are inextricably linked. This is the case whether democracy is seen as a bottom-up process in which voters mandate parties to deliver policies they want or as a representative process in which the governing parties decide policies in the interests of their voters. If governors take actions they deem necessary but unpopular, as long as they convincingly communicate their reasons for doing so, the link between representatives and represented is maintained.

For the first six centuries of Parliament's history there were no parties, for the absence of a secret ballot meant that MPs could intimidate constituents and hundreds of MPs were elected without a contest. The expansion of the franchise through nineteenth-century Reform Acts resulted in the electorate increasing into the millions, and nationwide party organisations were formed to link parties in Parliament with their supporters. Benjamin Disraeli sponsored the creation of a national union of local Conservative associations in 1867, and the National Liberal Federation was formed in 1877. The Labour Representation Committee of socialist societies and trade unions was founded in 1900. Since individuals qualified to vote could do so only if they registered, this gave parties the incentive to organise at the constituency level to make sure their eligible supporters could and did vote (Lowell, 1908: chapters 24–37).

This chapter shows how there has been an increasing detachment of Britons from the Conservative and Labour Parties but not from the broadly defined political process. Voter turnout has declined from its peak in the 1950s, and third-party competition has reduced the number of people voting for the two governing parties. Membership in the governing parties has fallen while parties on the left and right have recruited more members, and social media has made it possible for anyone to launch a site to mobilise people to support or oppose policies. While trust in many professionals is high, trust in politicians and government ministers is low. Partisan approval of prime ministers is distinctive in fluctuating widely within each leader's term of office more than between prime ministers. This is because approval is driven more by the performance of their government than by their personality.

Turnout declines

All citizens have the right to vote, but voting is not compulsory in Britain. Personal factors such as being on holiday or facing bad weather can lead people not to turn out, while making it easy for individuals to cast a postal ballot enables individuals to vote when it is personally convenient. If a party disappoints its usual supporters they may silently protest by not voting, while a very popular campaign may stimulate turnout among those who are normally disinclined to vote.

Who can vote

To cast a ballot an individual must have their name and constituency address included on the electoral register and, if asked at the polling station, produce an acceptable form of photographic identification. Compiling the electoral register is the responsibility of local government officials who annually circulate a questionnaire to every household asking for it to be returned listing all household members eligible to vote. As knowledge of English is not a requirement to vote in a British election, registration forms are distributed in 25 foreign languages ranging from Arabic to Urdu. Once an election is called it is now possible for unregistered individuals to register online. In 2024 more than 1.3 million people did so.

It is not illegal to be registered in more than one constituency. Since the date of an election is not fixed, students living away from home may register at their term-time address as well as at their parental home, and people who have a weekend second home may also register twice. It is only illegal if an individual votes twice in the same election. There is no requirement for people to de-register themselves if they move out of a constituency and register elsewhere. Nor does death automatically de-register an elector. The process results in millions more names being registered to vote than are legally able to do so.

A proportion of the eligible electorate is omitted from the electoral register. Householders can fail to return the registration form. Some eligible electors may want to keep their whereabouts private for personal reasons. Mobile tenants in short-term accommodation such as youths, the unemployed and immigrants are also more likely not to be registered. The Electoral Commission (2023) estimates that eight million people are either not registered to vote or no longer live at the address from which they have been registered to vote.

Laws affecting the right to vote have changed significantly in the post-war era. The right to vote by post was given to service personnel and a restricted number of ill and infirm citizens in 1948. Between 1950 and 1997 postal ballots accounted for between 1.6 per cent and 2.8 per cent of votes. The law was changed before the 2001 election so that postal voting became available on demand. Since then the percentage of voters given postal ballots has increased to 19.9 per cent in 2024.

The age qualifying a young person to vote was lowered to 18 in 1969. This increased the size of the electorate by about 8 per cent, albeit youths are less likely to register and turn out to vote. The expansion was undertaken by the Labour government in the full knowledge that young people were then more likely to vote Labour (Butler and Stokes, 1969: 60). However, the turnover of youths in the population can change how young people vote from one election to the next. A YouGov survey immediately after the 2024 election found that a majority of 18- to 24-year-old voters supported non-governing parties, especially the Greens, and were five times more likely to vote Labour than Conservative at that election. Keir Starmer's Labour government is proposing to lower the voting age to 16 for the 2029 general election.

An individual does not need to be a British citizen to vote for an MP; Commonwealth citizens and citizens of the Republic of Ireland can vote if they are resident in the United Kingdom. In Scotland and Wales, EU citizens have the right to vote in elections for the devolved parliaments and local elections and may vote in some English local government elections (Johnston, 2024). Since 1985 Britons living overseas have retained the right to vote in the constituency where they lived before emigrating. Few registered to vote until the 2016 Brexit referendum prompted 264,000 to do so. In 2024 the number of overseas voters was 191,000, about 6 per cent of the estimated three million Britons living abroad. As overseas voters are distributed among hundreds of constituencies, their impact on the choice of MPs is very small.

Who does vote

The formula for calculating official turnout is clear; the total number of valid votes cast in the United Kingdom divided by the total number of registered electors. However, as noted above, electoral registration is subject to errors of both omission and commission. Up to a point these errors cancel out, thereby subjecting official statements of turnout to an unknown but small margin of net error (cf. Rallings and Thrasher, 2012: xv–xvi).

Turnout was highest in the era of the two-party system, when a limited supply of housing made mobility difficult and elections tended to be close. Turnout was 83.9 per cent at the 1950 election, the highest since universal suffrage was introduced in the United Kingdom. It was almost as high in the following year although the number of candidates was the fewest in any democratic British election. During the period of two-party competition between 1950 and 1970, turnout never fell below 72 per cent and averaged 78 per cent.

The Liberal breakthrough in February 1974 produced a turnout of 78.8 per cent, a level that has not been reached subsequently. Notwithstanding the increase in the choice of parties and candidates, turnout has fallen since, reaching 59.4 per cent in 2001, the lowest since 1918. It then fluctuated between 61 per cent and 68 per cent in five elections up to 2019. Notwithstanding an increase in the number of candidates and six-party competition, in 2024 the total number of votes cast fell by more than 3.2 million from the preceding election, making the turnout of 59.7 per cent the second lowest in more than a century. In the 13 elections since 1974, turnout has averaged 70 per cent.

Governing parties lose members

The introduction of universal suffrage for men and women in 1918 trebled the size of the British electorate to twenty million, an average of more than 30,000 electors per constituency. By 1935 the Labour Party had 400,000 dues-paying members plus millions more whom trade unions affiliated whether they voted Labour or not. By contrast, the Conservative Party left it to their MPs and local worthies to organise support in their constituencies. Wealthy MPs could dispense with the need for a large constituency party by meeting its expenses themselves. In response to the party's defeat at the 1945 election, Lord Woolton, a successful retailer turned party chairman, converted the Conservative Party into a mass-membership organisation of individual supporters. While parties differ in their definition of members, the common feature is that their records are imperfect. Hence, even precise numbers are best treated as estimates of membership at a given point of time (Burton and Tunnicliffe, 2022).

At the peak of party membership in the early 1950s, the Conservatives claimed 2.8 million individual members. The Labour Party reached a peak of one million individual members in 1952 and 6.5 million affiliated trade union members in 1979. Party membership then began to fall gradually. By 1981 individual membership in the Labour Party was below its 1939 level. Notwithstanding the political success of Margaret Thatcher in mobilising electoral support, the Conservative Party's undocumented membership fell to an estimated 1.2 million in the 1980s and to less than half a million by 1997 (Butler and Butler, 2011: 158f, 175ff; Whiteley, 2009). When the Social Democratic Party broke away from the Labour Party it introduced membership paid to its national organisation by credit card. This gave the

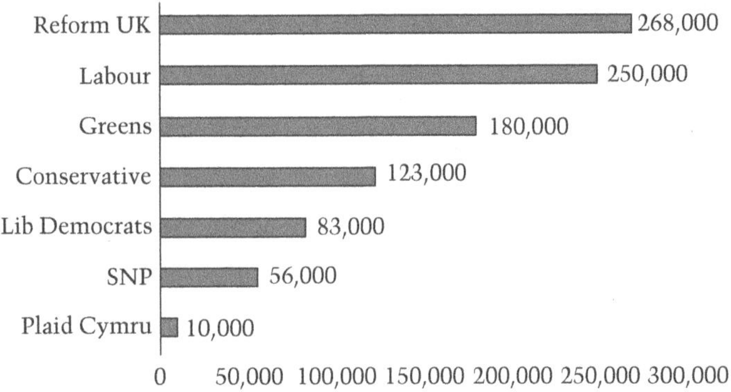

Figure 2.1 Party membership
Source: Party websites. https://en.wikipedia.org/wiki/Political_party_affiliation_in_the_United_Kingdom Accessed 12 December 2025.

party headquarters the capacity to control the flow of information to members and freed MPs from pressures by left-wing constituency party activists (Crewe and King, 1995: chapter 13).

Today, fewer than 2 per cent of the electorate belong to a political party. The reported membership of Reform UK, 268,000, has surpassed that of the Labour Party (Figure 2.1). One reason is that Nigel Farage's party has made aggressive and skilled use of social media to attract support (Reform UK, 2026). Secondly, Labour Party membership has fallen by one-third in reaction to the actions of the Starmer government (see chapter 5). The Green Party now ranks third in membership thanks to a surge in support under Zack Polanski's leadership. The Conservative Party's membership is a shadow of its former self.

A party's most committed supporters not only vote for it but also pay dues. On this criterion, Scottish National Party voters are the most committed. Its 56,000 members are equal to 8 per cent of its vote at the 2024 general election, and Plaid Cymru's membership is 5.5 per cent of its vote. Reform UK's membership in autumn 2025 is equivalent to 6.3 per cent of its 2024 vote, and 3 per cent of its current support in the polls. Similarly, the Green Party's current membership is about 4 per cent of its current poll support. The two governing parties each have fewer committed members. Labour's estimated membership is now about 2.5 per cent of its vote at the last election. The Conservative Party has the lowest proportion of voters sufficiently committed to become party members, 1.8 per cent of its 2024 vote.

A big majority of party members limit their engagement to paying dues (Bale, Webb and Poletti, 2019). Active members can focus on local government issues and become councillors. Each constituency party can send delegates to the party's national conference and speak and vote on resolutions. The Labour leadership almost invariably wins conference debates, but only after negotiating with trade union leaders who can command blocs of votes. A Conservative conference chair can tell vocal members they have heard their views and ask them to withdraw controversial motions in deference to the knowledge of the parliamentary leadership.

In response to claims that the choice of party leader by a parliamentary caucus was undemocratic, party members have been given the power to make the final choice of the party leader, starting in 1983 with the Labour Party establishing an electoral college of trade unions, MPs and party members (Butler and Butler, 2011: 164ff). Constituency party members endorsed the winner until 2010, when Ed Miliband was elected party leader thanks to substantial support from trade unions overcoming majority support from party members and MPs for his brother, David Miliband. After the electoral college was abolished, Jeremy Corbyn was elected with 59 per cent of members' votes; Andy Burnham came second. In 2020 Keir Starmer won 56 per cent of the vote in what was then an electorate of 784,000 members.

Since 2001 the Conservative Party leader has been chosen in a two-stage process in which MPs first ballot on a multiplicity of candidates and the top two then face a vote of party members; the winning candidate becomes the party leader. Two of the eight leadership contests have resulted in the first choice of MPs being rejected by party members in favour of MPs' second choice. In this way Iain Duncan Smith bested Ken Clarke in 2005, and Liz Truss became prime minister in 2017 instead of the MPs' favourite, Rishi Sunak. After the party's 2024 election defeat, Kemi Badenoch was elected party leader over Robert Jenrick in a ballot in which 94,000 party members voted.

Alternative forms of political communication

Civil society institutions have long been important sources of party support. In late Victorian times Church of England and nonconformist church-goers voted for the Conservative and Liberal Parties respectively, and trade unions provided the money and organisation to create the Labour Party. Today, both churches and trade unions have lost millions of members, but civil society institutions are numerous and active, while usually avoiding close partisan ties. There are thousands of community organisations involved in everything from sports clubs to choirs. When they seek to advance their interests through the policy process, they usually emphasise that they are non-political in the sense of having no ties to a political party. The membership of civil society institutions concerned with community and national issues exceeds by far the membership of parties. For example, the Royal Horticultural Society has more than half a million individual members and the National Council for Voluntary Organisations has more than 17,000 institutional members in England.

In the 1950s the daily press was the only media institution bringing political news to the electorate and claimed to represent its readers' views. The BBC interpreted impartiality as under-reporting different political views for fear of appearing to take political sides. Newspapers not only expressed partisan views in print but also in face-to-face private meetings with party leaders seeking press backing. In 1950 pro-Conservative papers, led by the *Daily Express*, had a print circulation of 7.5 million and pro-Labour papers, led by the *Daily Mirror*, a circulation of 6.6 million (Butler and Butler, 2011: 571). Thus, 45 per cent of the electorate bought a partisan paper and, since many papers had more than one reader, a big majority of voters received daily news of political activities.

The top-down dissemination of political news through the press has lost its monopoly of political communication. The introduction of commercial television from 1955 produced competition for audiences, with commercial stations initiating the coverage of controversial news, which the BBC then followed. The decades since have seen a big increase in the number of broadcasting outlets. The development of the internet and digitisation have greatly multiplied both the quantity and the variety of ways in which political news and views are communicated. At the click of a mouse, an interested viewer can today compare coverage of the same issue by multiple print, broadcast and internet sources.

A YouGov study two weeks before the 2024 election found that respondents got their political news from an average of 2.5 sources. Television and radio together accounted for two-fifths of sources mentioned. Print and online newspapers accounted for just over one-fifth of mentions, as did a variety of electronic sources such as websites and podcasts. Social media sites originating independently of well-organised institutions accounted for one-sixth of political news and views. There are radical age differences in the source of news. Whereas 90 per cent of those over the age of 75 rely on broadcast content, only one-quarter of those under 35 do so (Ofcom, 2025).

Beginning with the 1959 election, party headquarters began appealing to voters through advertising in the mass media (Rose, 1967). Centralisation frees the party leadership from relying on constituency party members to make contact with voters because party headquarters can send its own messages to millions of voters. It also raises the prominence of the party's leader, who is pictured in far more advertisements and media stories than the party's other front-bench MPs. Since the cost of national advertising cannot be met through membership dues, parties have turned to soliciting donations denominated in fractions of a million or more from a small number of rich supporters who share their views and prize access to the powerful. This has freed Labour leaders from exclusive reliance on trade unions for money.

An incidental consequence of turning to professional public relations is that it has increased the attention that party strategists give to blocs of voters whose support could tip first-past-the-post results their way. This feeds back to influence the choice of slogans, the phrasing of messages and policy presentation and priorities. Once a party is in government, polls continuously feed Downing Street with evidence of how the government's policies and leadership are being evaluated by the electorate. However, this information does not provide the public funds to pay for popular policies. Nor can the appearance of party leaders be easily changed. For example, the thousands of pounds given by a supporter to buy clothes and glasses to smarten up Keir Starmer did nothing to boost his rating with the electorate.

Social media also offers the means for groups independent of parties to express their views to target audiences such as young people. Political influencers use YouTube, podcasts and other online resources to provide a steady flow of views that promote viewpoints not on the political agenda at Westminster. MPs and their staff who follow the internet are exposed to a much wider range of issues than they would hear about in discussions within their normal circle of partisan contacts. Ordinary people who get views and news from social media, with the former often disguised as the latter, can have their political outlook shaped or reinforced by online communication. In form this is a radical change from talking about public affairs with friends and workmates. Whether online or face to face, the result of such conversations can be the same: the reinforcement of an individual's political views.

Political trust low

In a society with a population of almost seventy million, the people cannot govern. They must put their trust in institutions and office-holders who make and deliver public policies. This is especially so in Britain, given the lack of a written constitution with laws designed to make politicians behave in a trustworthy manner. In the past the aristocratic origins of governors encouraged their deferential subjects to trust a government of men. The fear of founders of the Labour Party that the law would be used to restrict working-class institutions resulted in the Labour government of Harold Wilson being unable to bring in legislation intended to improve industrial relations, leaving the task of doing so to the government of Margaret Thatcher.

Democratic elections give the tens of millions who vote the chance to decide which party and which people will govern in their name. The standards that ordinary people use to decide whether British politicians are trustworthy are not the laws that courts use, but subjective impressions gleaned from multiple sources described in the previous section. In addition, at Prime Minister's Question Time in the Commons and during election campaigns the Labour and Conservative Parties seek to encourage distrust in their opponents as much as trust in themselves. In two-party competition for control of government, power can be won by the party that is least distrusted.

Lack of political trust

For more than forty years Ipsos has maintained a Veracity Index asking a question about how much people trust professional politicians and non-political professionals: *Now I will read you a list of different types of people. For each would you tell me if you generally trust them to tell the truth or not?*

Over the decades trust in politicians to tell the truth has always been low, whichever party was in government. It has fluctuated up and down by small and often statistically insignificant amounts around a long-term mean of fewer than 20 per cent trusting politicians. Trust stood at 18 per cent in 1986 and rose to a relative high of 23 per cent in 1999. The disclosure of the way in which MPs were abusing expense claims led trust to drop to 13 per cent in 2009. Since then, trust has

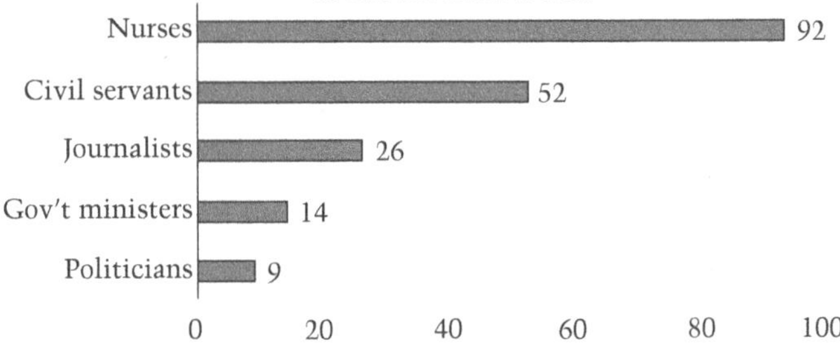

Figure 2.2 Low trust in professional politicians (%)
Source: https://www.ipsos.com/en-uk/ipsos-veracity-index-2025. Consulted 12 December 2025.

fluctuated at an even lower level. Trust in politicians hit a low of 9 per cent in 2023, reflecting Boris Johnson's sleaze and Liz Truss's incompetence as prime minister; it is still that low in 2025 (Figure 2.2).

Trust in government ministers telling the truth is also lacking. At its relative highest, it was 25 per cent during Tony Blair's government; it then fell along with trust in MPs in 2009. A mild recovery followed before it dropped again when Boris Johnson became prime minister. The record low in trust in ministers, 10 per cent, was reached in 2023. The pattern indicates that government ministers are seen as politicians rather than benefiting from their positions as public officials.

The 1980s television political satire sitcom *Yes, Minister* showed the methods that Whitehall civil servants can use to put brakes on what ministers want to do that they deem ill advised, and both Labour and

Conservative prime ministers have expressed distrust in civil servants, whom they see as obstacles to their delivery of election promises. The view of ordinary people is different. The civil servants whom the mass of the public deals with are public officials delivering public services locally. These officials are bureaucrats charged with administering laws impersonally before deciding whether or not a claimant is eligible to receive a benefit. This gives them the reputation of acting fairly rather than behaving like a politician who promises to deliver a service that never arrives.

Public opinion has increasingly diverged in its view of civil servants as compared with politicians and ministers. Trust in officials rose from 37 per cent in 1992 and hit a high of 65 per cent trusting civil servants in 2008. Trust has since declined and ministers of both governing parties and Nigel Farage have attacked civil servants as part of the 'deep state' allegedly obstructing elected politicians from working their will while in government. Nonetheless, trust in civil servants is 43 percentage points higher than trust in politicians.

The distrust that ordinary people show in politicians is not because they are suspicious of all kinds of people; it is specific to elected officials. Popular discrimination is shown by the very wide range of ratings that Veracity Index respondents give to different professions (Figure 2.2). At the top are nurses, trusted by 92 per cent, followed by engineers and doctors. Fourteen professions, including civil servants, are trusted by at least 50 per cent of Britons. Fewer than half trust 11 different groups such as estate agents, journalists and advertising executives. Government ministers and politicians are lowest in trust among more than two dozen professions.

While distrust in politicians contradicts the idealistic assumption that elected representatives will do the right thing, it is in keeping with the view of one of the authors of the American Constitution, James Madison. He argued that if people were angels no government would be needed, but as this is not the case a constitution must establish institutions that control governors as well as the governed. This was done by an intricate system of institutional checks and balances between the presidency, Congress and the courts. While Donald Trump has stretched institutional constraints to the breaking point, they still put more limitations on his behaviour than are found in the regimes of the dictators Trump admires.

Free competitive elections institutionalise the power of Britons to hold distrusted politicians accountable. People can vote to turn out of office a group of politicians seen as lacking both ethics and effectiveness. The threat of losing office, which can be revealed regularly by opinion polls, is an incentive to governors to try to gain popular confidence. The way in which individual ministers perform in the House of Commons threatens those who lose the trust of their party's MPs with being sacked by the prime minister. Conversations between back-benchers in the bars and meeting rooms of the Commons and through WhatsApp messages can be used to by MPs to hold to account a party leader trusted only to lead the party to defeat.

2.3 Satisfaction with prime minister declines

The prime minister has a role in both the dignified and the efficient parts of British government. Television has made the prime minister's personality and the door of 10 Downing Street dignified symbols of government. References to Her or His Majesty's Government have been replaced by terms such as Boris Johnson's government or Keir Starmer's government. Focusing on the prime minister vastly oversimplifies their engagement with the effective machinery of government.

At the same time opposition parties are seeking to stir up dissatisfaction with the prime minister as part of their campaign to gain control of government. Moreover, the scale and diversity of print, broadcast and social media offer much more scope for disparaging the prime minister than weekly question time in the House of Commons. The journalists' motto – Names make news – has a corollary: Bad news about a prime minister makes headline news.

Evaluation by performance, not personality

One theory emphasises the prime minister's personality as the chief determinant of their popular approval. Since their personality is relatively fixed, this implies that a prime minister's popularity will be relatively constant during their period in office. By contrast, institutional theories emphasise that the reputation of a prime minister depends on their performance and that of the government they head. This approach suggests that a prime minister's approval should fluctuate up and down during their term of office or, in the worst case, follow a trend down from the height of popularity on entering Downing Street to the point at which they leave.

Unlike quinquennial elections, opinion polls can continuously register the public's view of the prime minister of the day. In 1945 the Gallup Poll started measuring public opinion about the prime minister by asking: *Are you satisfied or dissatisfied with [name] as Prime Minister?* Gallup repeated this question almost every month from 1955 until 1999; Ipsos has been regularly tracking prime ministerial satisfaction since then. Thus, 80 years of comparative data about public approval of the 18 occupants of Number 10 is available to test how much satisfaction varies between prime ministers and how much it varies within the period when a politician is prime minister.

Even though every prime minister has won office with less than half the vote, almost three-quarters have been popular with a majority of the electorate at some point while in office (Table 2.1). Three prime ministers – Anthony Eden in 1955, Harold Macmillan in 1960 and Tony Blair in 1997 – have each satisfied more than 70 per cent of the electorate in at least one monthly poll. Two were old-fashioned Conservatives born when Victoria was queen while Tony Blair rejected the past, styling himself New Labour. Satisfaction up to half again more than the vote for the prime minister's party shows that many Britons can differentiate between their partisan vote and how they evaluate the head of government.

Table 2.1 Highs and lows in satisfaction with prime ministers (%)

	High	Low	Range
Clement Attlee	66	37	29
Winston Churchill	56	48	8
Anthony Eden	73	41	32
Harold Macmillan	79	30	49
Sir Alec Douglas-Home	48	42	6
Harold Wilson 1964–70	69	27	42
Edward Heath	45	31	14
Harold Wilson 1974–76	53	40	13
Jim Callaghan	59	33	26
Margaret Thatcher	53	23	30
John Major	59	18	41
Tony Blair	75	23	52
Gordon Brown	41	21	20
David Cameron	57	31	26
Theresa May	56	25	31
Boris Johnson	52	24	28
Liz Truss	27	16	11
Rishi Sunak	32	16	16
Keir Starmer	38	13	25

Sources: Rose (1995: 280); www.ipsos.com/en-uk/political-monitor-satisfaction-ratings-1997-present

The popularity experienced by each prime minister is not related to their personality. Clement Attlee was unprepossessing; as the House of Commons quip put it, 'An empty taxi drew up and Clement Attlee got out.' Nonetheless, Attlee satisfied two-thirds of the electorate at his peak. The performance of the 1945–51

Labour government explains why Attlee was rated so highly. Peak satisfaction with Attlee was higher than with 14 other prime ministers, including such personable figures as Jim Callaghan, nicknamed Sunny Jim, and Boris Johnson. This suggests that, if Keir Starmer wants to be popular, he does not need to change his personality; he needs to improve the performance of his government.

Six prime ministers have failed to be endorsed by as much as half the public at any time during their stay in Downing Street, beginning with Sir Alec Douglas-Home during his short-lived premiership in 1963–64. Liz Truss and Rishi Sunak failed to achieve the support of one-third of the voters in at least one monthly poll. Of this group only Ted Heath and Keir Starmer gained office by winning a general election. Five were subsequently defeated when they sought election on the basis of their performance in office. Starmer has yet to be tested.

Notwithstanding the personality of a party leader remaining constant, their political performance is variable, as they sometimes react successfully to challenges and sometimes fail to do so. The influence of the government's performance is shown by every prime minister failing to get the approval of half the electorate at some point during their tenure. Keir Starmer has achieved the lowest satisfaction rating of any prime minister; in November 2025 it was down to 13 per cent. This was below the level of Rishi Sunak and Liz Truss in the previous Conservative government, as well as John Major three decades earlier. Even prime ministers who have registered peak levels of satisfaction have also slumped greatly. By the time he left office Tony Blair satisfied less than a quarter of the electorate and Harold Macmillan at his lowest satisfied less than one-third of Britons.

Ironically, the higher the level of satisfaction a prime minister achieved, the more their popularity can fall. Satisfaction with Tony Blair fell 52 percentage points by the time he left office, and Harold Macmillan's fell 49 percentage points. By contrast, prime ministers who never succeeded in gaining much public satisfaction saw their ratings drop much less. That of Liz Truss fell only 11 percentage points from her 'high' of 27 per cent and that of her unpopular successor Rishi Sunak fell only 16 percentage points.

Satisfaction with Opposition leaders

Since the Gallup Poll began asking about approval of the Opposition leader in 1956, a total of 18 MPs have been leaders of the official Opposition. Five have gone on to become prime minister – Harold Wilson, Margaret Thatcher, Tony Blair, David Cameron and Keir Starmer (Table 2.2). Six Labour leaders never became prime minister, and three 21st-century Conservative leaders have so far experienced the same fate.

Opposition leaders struggle to compete with the prime minister for attention in the media; sometimes a third or more of respondents have no opinion on their performance. Nonetheless, ten Opposition leaders at some point have been endorsed by at least half the electorate. At their highest point Tony Blair and Harold

Table 2.2 Highs and lows in satisfaction with Opposition leaders (%)

	High	Low	Range
Hugh Gaitskell	57	32	25
[1]Harold Wilson 1963–64	67	44	22
[2]Sir Alec Douglas-Home	41	32	9
[2]Edward Heath 1965–70	51	24	27
[2]Harold Wilson 1970–74	66	38	28
[2]Edward Heath	38	29	9
[1]Margaret Thatcher	64	31	33
[2]Jim Callaghan	63	46	17
Michael Foot	38	9	29
Neil Kinnock	58	26	32
John Smith	53	43	10
[1]Tony Blair	68	46	22
William Hague	29	12	17
Iain Duncan Smith	27	15	12
Michael Howard	31	22	9
[1]David Cameron	52	23	29
Ed Miliband	41	21	20
Jeremy Corbyn	43	16	27
[1]Keir Starmer	51	22	29
Kemi Badenoch	23	11	12

Notes:
[1]Subsequently prime minister.
[2]Previously prime minister.
Sources: Rose (1995: 280); www.ipsos.com/en-uk/political-monitor-satisfaction-ratings-1997-present

Wilson each satisfied two-thirds of respondents, giving them big leads over the prime minister of the day. Six highly popular Opposition leaders had been or went on to become prime minister. Neil Kinnock was the only leader in this group who did not become prime minister.

Unsurprisingly, Opposition leaders who never satisfy a majority tend not to win the key to Number 10. Ted Heath, at best approved by only 38 per cent, was the one exception, besting the popular Harold Wilson in 1970 because of the Labour government's unsatisfactory performance in managing the economy.

The failure of rapid changes of leaders to bring quick electoral success to the official Opposition reflects the slight influence that the leader has on the electorate (King, 2002). Opposition leaders take office in a party that has been rejected by the electorate because of its unsatisfactory performance. Changing leaders can do little if the new leader heads a party confused about why it was not in government. Michael Foot leading a Labour Party competing with the breakaway SDP as well as the Tories had a satisfaction rating as low as 9 per cent; at best it was only 38 per cent. It took four changes of leadership before David Cameron could 'de-toxify' the Conservative Party and return it to Downing Street. Kemi Badenoch is now struggling to shed the negative reputation of the Conservative government of which she was a minister. After losing the 2010 election Labour tried three different leaders before the Conservative government's unpopularity made Opposition leader Keir Starmer the prime minister.

An Opposition leader may create conditions for gaining votes by reforming their party. Margaret Thatcher filled the vacuum created by the collapse of the Heath government's economic policy with a very different ideology. Tony Blair rebranded the Labour Party as New Labour. Keir Starmer positioned Labour as moving to the political centre by expelling his predecessor, Jeremy Corbyn.

Evaluations of leaders of non-governing parties are not comparable since they are not seen as a potential prime minister. When a Liberal Democratic leader is evaluated as a prime minister rather than as the leader of a non-governing party, their rating drops sharply. For example, when respondents were asked to evaluate Paddy Ashdown as party leader before the 1997 election, he was given a positive rating by 67 per cent of respondents. However, in reply to a question about who would make the best prime minister, only 12 per cent endorsed Ashdown.

Satisfaction with the choice of leaders

In optimal circumstances, satisfaction with the leaders of governing parties ought to add up to 100 per cent, as the popularity of one leader offsets the unpopularity of the other. However, if the unpopularity of one leader is matched by an unsatisfactory rating for the other, their combined endorsement will fall below 100 per cent. In that case, some voters will either have to cast a vote for a lesser evil or vote for a party whose leader has no chance of becoming prime minister.

Since evaluations of the Labour and Conservative leaders are independent of each other, satisfaction with the two leaders competing for Downing Street can add up to more than 100 per cent. In the era of two-party competition, the combined approval rating of Conservative and Labour leaders went as high as 126 per cent when Harold Macmillan was the Conservative prime minister and as high as 113 per cent when Harold Wilson was the Labour prime minister. It was also high when John Major was prime minister, due to the popularity of Opposition leader Tony Blair (Rose, 1995: table 5).

Combined support has not reached 100 per cent since 1997. In part this reflects the weak standing of Conservative and Labour Opposition leaders, reinforced by Tony Blair's successors as prime ministers never gaining his level of popular satisfaction; four of the eight never being endorsed by as much as half the electorate. Further, when Rishi Sunak had the approval of only 16 per cent in 2024, adding Keir Starmer's rating brought the combined approval of the two candidates for Downing Street up to just 41 per cent.

In the long run there has been a reduction in popular approval of prime ministers and of leaders of the official Opposition as well as in the combined support for the Labour and Conservative party leaders. However, it has been not a steady decline, but a ratchet-like movement down and up and then down again. This indicates that the decline is a tendency, rather than a trend.

Detachment differs between forms of engagement

The extent to which Britons are becoming detached from party politics differs between forms of engagement. The two-party share of the national vote has fallen by 39 percentage points between a high mark in 1951 and a low in 2024. The bulk of that loss was due to voters shifting their support from one of the two governing parties to one or another non-governing party The fall in turnout of only 7 percentage points in the period indicates that the percentage of confirmed non-voters in the electorate is low.

The direction of change in party membership depends on the party. Membership in the two governing parties has plummeted. The Conservative Party now averages about two hundred members per constituency when it used to average more than two thousand. Trade union membership in the Labour Party has fallen greatly from the millions affiliated by trade union headquarters. Non-governing parties on the right and the left, led by Reform UK and the Green Party, are now attracting many new members. Bottom-up communication outside the control of political parties has flourished with the development of the internet and social media.

Trust in politicians and government ministers has never been high. Due to enduring scepticism, there has been only a small trend downwards. By contrast, a majority of Britons trust civil servants, who are bureaucratic checks on partisan politicians unconstrained by a written constitution. The evaluation of party leaders has always fluctuated within each leader's time in Downing Street, depending on the performance of the government they head. The development of the hybrid three-party system has created party leaders who cannot be held responsible for the performance of government, because they have never been in control of government. This has helped figures such as Ed Davey and Nigel Farage when compared with governing party leaders such as Keir Starmer and Kemi Badenoch.

It is misleading to describe the great majority of people who do not vote at a particular election as politically alienated; they are not consistent non-voters. Most people who do not vote at a particular election do so for a variety of reasons such as ill health, being on holiday, lack of political interest or thinking that their vote will make no difference in their constituency (Ledgerwood and Lally, 2024). In the course of their lifetime, the average elector will have the opportunity to vote in more than a dozen elections. If they turn out to vote at the same 70 per cent rate of average turnout, they will vote in eight or more elections. In other words, it is misleading to label such people as non-voters; they are people who usually vote when a general election is held.

Citations

Bale, Tim, Webb, Paul and Poletti, Monica, 2019. *Footsoldiers: Political Party Membership in the 21st Century*. London: Routledge.

Burton, Matthew and Tunnicliffe, Richard, 2022. *Membership in Political Parties in Britain*. London: House of Commons Library Research Briefing.

Butler, David and Butler, Gareth, 2011. *British Political Facts*. London: Palgrave Macmillan, 10th edition.

Butler, David and Stokes, Donald, 1969. *Political Change in Britain*. London: Macmillan.

Crewe, Ivor and King, Anthony, 1995. *SDP: The Birth, Life and Death of the Social Democratic Party*. Oxford: Oxford University Press.

Electoral Commission, 2023. 'Explore the data: who is and who isn't registered to vote?', www.electoralcommission.org.uk/who-is-registered. Accessed 21 December 2025.

Johnston, Neil, 2024. *Who Can Vote at a British Election?* London: House of Commons Library Research Briefing.

King, Anthony, ed., 2002. *Leaders' Personalities and the Outcomes of Democratic Elections*. Oxford: Oxford University Press.

Ledgerwood, Emmeline and Lally, Claire, 2024. *Election Turnout: Why Do Some People Not Vote?* London: Parliamentary Office of Science and Technology (POST).

Lowell, A. Lawrence, 1908. *The Government of England*. London: Macmillan, 2 vols.

Ofcom, 2025. 'Media nations: UK 2025', www.ofcom.org.uk. Accessed 30 July 2025.

Rallings, Colin and Thrasher, Michael, 2012. *British Electoral Facts, 1832–2012*. London: Biteback.

Reform UK, 2026. 'Membership', https://www.reformparty.uk/membership. Accessed 26 January 2026.

Rose, Richard, 1967. *Influencing Voters: A Study in Campaign Rationality*. London: Faber & Faber.

Rose, Richard, 1995. 'A crisis of confidence in British party leaders?', *Contemporary Record*, 9, 2, 273–293.

Whiteley, Paul, 2009. 'Where have all the members gone? The dynamics of party membership in Britain', *Parliamentary Affairs*, 62, 2, 242–257.

3
Voters free to choose

Britons have definitely not given up on elections: more than two-thirds think it is a duty to vote, and a substantial majority do so whenever a general election is called (YouGov, 2022). Detachment from governing parties means that people are now free to choose which party they vote for or against, instead of having their vote determined by inherited ties of class or party identification. Moreover, a steady flow of opinion polls shows that a big election victory can be undermined if the governing party's performance in office disappoints. Politicians do not own their votes but only receive them on loan until the next election.

Instead of having a lifetime party identification, many electors are now open-minded about switching their vote between parties, including new parties such as Reform UK. While a person can vote for only one party at a given general election, individuals are becoming multi-party voters as they switch between parties from one general election to the next. Variations in the governing party's performance and events beyond its control create dynamic changes in party competition.

Even if a party wins few seats in Parliament, as is the case with the Green Party and Plaid Cymru, it can persist for decades. Moreover, there is always the possibility of disruption giving it the opportunity to become relevant, as happens when British voters turn their backs on both governing parties.

The extent to which voters have become choosy rather than party loyalists is documented in the pages that follow. The first section shows the decline in the influence of class on voting behaviour. The second shows the erosion of a party identification inherited from parents by big changes in education and social mobility and by actions of parties. Opinion polls and by-election results show that more than one-third of those who voted Labour can abandon it within a year of it taking office. While the Labour and Conservative Parties maintain their left–right identities, the values of voters are now multi-dimensional. The chapter concludes by contrasting voters who are open-minded about parties with long-term loyalists.

Class no longer influential

In the days of the two-party British system, the choice of voters was treated as a reflection of their social class. In the words of Peter Pulzer (1967: 98), 'Class is the basis of British party politics; all else is embellishment and detail.' In its simplest form, this postulated that middle-class voters would support the Conservatives and working-class voters would vote Labour. However, if that had been the case the Labour Party would have won every election since 1918, when the working class was a majority of the electorate.

Sociological reductionism ignores the effort sophisticated politicians have made to win elections by mobilising supporters across class lines. The late nineteenth-century Conservative prime minister Benjamin Disraeli saw newly enfranchised working-class voters as silent 'angels in marble' trusting aristocratic Conservative leaders. The preamble of the 1918 Labour Party constitution rejected the Marxist idea of class conflict. It described Labour as an inclusive party for workers by hand or by brain, then as now almost all of the electorate. Harold Macmillan promoted one-nation Conservatism, emphasising policies with a cross-class appeal such as ownership of a car and a house (McKenzie and Silver, 1968).

Dividing the population into classes by occupation ignores the fact that many people have a mixture of middle-class and working-class characteristics such as income, occupation, education, trade union membership, ethnicity and race (Rose, 1968). Social and economic change is diminishing the proportion of the electorate that is exclusively middle-class or working-class on all these characteristics. Moreover, people are free to decide subjectively which class they identify with. Keir Starmer, an upper-middle-class barrister by occupation, often invokes his father's skilled working-class occupation to identify himself with working people, a term that embraces people of all occupational classes.

The changing relationship between class and voting can be tracked with Gallup Poll and YouGov surveys from 1950 to the present (Table 3.1). A scale developed by market research agencies divides the population into two groups based on their occupation, employment and income. The ABC1 group ranges from higher professional and managerial roles considered upper middle-class, through intermediate white-collar positions, to clerical and related roles associated with lower middle-class status. The C2DE working-class group consists of skilled, semi-skilled and unskilled workers, pensioners and others relying on state social welfare benefits for their income (Office of National Statistics, 2026).

The benefit the Labour and Conservative Parties gain from class-based voting is a function of two factors: the support each party gains from its favoured class and the size of each class in the electorate. In the first two decades after the Second World War more than two-thirds of the electorate was working-class. However, changes in the economy and in society gradually reduced the size of this group so that by the year 2000 the occupationally middle-class constituted half the electorate. In 2024 YouGov's massive post-election survey assigned 57 per cent of respondents to the middle-class ABC1 group.

The 1950 election divided voters into two almost equal groups of Labour and Conservative voters; it also divided voters by class. Among middle-class voters, the Conservatives had a more than four to one lead over Labour. Among working-class voters, Labour was in the lead by less than two to one over the Conservatives (Table 3.1). When Harold Wilson led Labour to a big victory in 1966 he did it by increasing Labour support

Table 3.1 Decline in class voting 1950–2024 (%)

	1950		1974		2019		2024	
	Middle	Work	Middle	Work	Middle	Work	Middle	Work
Labour	17	55	23	52	31	36	36	33
Conservative	69	34	59	33	45	45	26	23
	—	—	—	—	—	—	—	—
Difference in %								
Lab–Con	−52	21	−36	19	−14	−9	10	10

Notes: Middle class: ABC1. Working class: C2DE. Totals do not add to 100 per cent because votes for other parties are not shown.
Source: Calculated by the author from Gallup (1976: 206f) and YouGov survey, 5–8 July 2024.

among a minority of the middle class as well as among working-class voters.

In the first three-party election in 1974, both governing parties lost support among their favoured class. The Conservatives benefited from an 11 percentage point increase in the size of the middle class since 1950, while social change worked to the disadvantage of Labour as the size of the working class dropped. The Liberals drew their minority support evenly from across class lines. The relationship between party and class was disrupted when the Social Democratic Party broke away from the Labour Party to form an alliance with the Liberals. In 1983 the Labour Party and the SDP–Liberal Alliance divided a majority of the working-class vote. This enabled the Conservatives to win a plurality of working-class votes (Rose and McAllister, 1986: table 3.2).

The 2016 referendum on Britain's membership in the European Union was an issue quite different from the class division described by Pulzer. It also made attitudes towards immigration salient (Goodwin and Milazzo, 2017). In the 2019 election that followed, Boris Johnson stressed that the Conservatives were the party that would 'get Brexit done'. This resulted in the Conservatives coming first among both middle-class and working-class voters with 45 per cent of the vote (Hawkins and Loft, 2020: 55).

By the 2024 election Brexit had fallen from being first among issues to being the least important issue to voters. This made it theoretically possible for class once again to become a major dividing line in the electorate. However, this did not happen. Given six-party competition, Labour came first among both middle-class and working-class voters, but did not win a majority in either class. Moreover, its 36 per cent share of middle-class respondents was 3 percentage points more than its share of the working-class vote (Table 3.1).

Age and education have replaced class as the major social division in the electorate (cf. Gallup, 1976: 168f). Among young voters, 41 per cent voted Labour at the 2024 election compared to 8 per cent Conservative. Among voters age 65 or above, the opposite was the case: 42 per cent chose the Conservatives compared to 22 per cent voting Labour. Among the third of voters with higher education, Labour gained 42 per cent of the vote as against 18 per cent voting Conservative. Among those with a minimum of education, the Conservatives were favoured by a margin of 31 per cent of the vote as against 28 per cent Labour.

Party identification weakens

The first instinct of Labour leaders confronted with evidence that class does not determine voting has been to search for an alternative definition of class. The search became a major priority after the Labour Party, contrary to the expectation of its leader Hugh Gaitskell, lost the 1959 election (cf. Abrams and Rose, 1960). It continues with Keir Starmer, who won an election with 10 per cent less of the working-class vote than Gaitskell had secured in losing an election half a century before. When I challenged a leading Gaitskell adviser, Anthony Crosland, at an Oxford seminar in 1960 by saying class was not the chief determinant of voting, he sharply replied: 'If not class, what does influence voters?' Drawing on a new social psychological theory of American voting (Campbell et al., 1960), I replied: 'Party identification'. Everyone laughed; they thought this was a tautology. However, in the United States it is not; it provides a political identity that people with all kinds of social identities can use when marking their ballot for every office from president to sheriff and dog-catcher.

Party identification in theory and practice

In its original form the theory of party identification was even more deterministic than class theories of voting. It postulated that individuals begin to develop a party identification in childhood by following their parents. Thus, when a general election is called, as long as the parties remain the same, youthful voters do not need to have an interest in or knowledge of politics to cast their first vote. They simply vote as their parents did. The inter-generational transmission of party loyalties from parents to children is part of a process of youthful socialisation rather than a choice based on political knowledge and adult experience. In so far as party identification is widespread in a society, it creates electoral stability, as people vote for the party they identify with regardless of what it does. In introducing the concept of party identification in Britain, David Butler and Donald Stokes (1974: 49) quoted approvingly a Gilbert and Sullivan song, 'Nature does contrive that every boy and every gal that's born into the world alive is either a little Liberal or else a little Conservative.'

The British Election Study (BES) measures party identification by asking a sample of voters: *Generally speaking, do you usually think of yourself as a Conservative, Labour or Liberal or what?* If a choice is made, a follow-up question is asked about whether the respondent feels very strongly, fairly strongly or not very strongly affiliated with their party. The word 'feeling' emphasises psychological attachment to a party. This does not require a voter to agree with or even know their party's policies (Clarke and Stewart, 1998).

When Butler and Stokes (1969) first asked Britons about their party identification in 1964, a total of 92 per cent identified with a political party, including 81 per cent identifying with either Labour or the Conservative Party. The introduction of a three-party system of party competition in 1974 reduced identification with the two governing parties by 6 percentage points. At the 1983 election the Social Democratic Party break with Labour reduced two-party identification to 67 per cent. Tony Blair's launch of New Labour did not cause an immediate change in party identification but after a Conservative–Liberal Democrat coalition gained office the proportion not identifying with any party had more than doubled to 22 per cent. Following the Brexit referendum, YouGov found in 2019 that one-third of the electorate did not identify with any party, a total that has increased since.

The decline in identification with the two governing parties reached a peak during the 2024 election campaign. The BES survey found that only 44 per cent of respondents said they identified with either the Labour or the Conservative Parties, a fall of 37 percentage points since the question was first asked. This total was augmented by an additional 19 per cent identifying with parties that did not exist when a majority of their parents first voted.

Describing party identification as inherited from parents ignores relevant evidence. Some people do not know their parents' party preference, and some receive conflicting cues from parents who vote for different parties. Divorce and re-marriage complicate the meaning of parents. Discontinuity in parties on the ballot since parents started voting has further reduced inter-generational influence. In Labour families, 81 per cent of those interviewed in 1963 said they were Labour voters; in 2025 only 33 per cent were Labour supporters. In Conservative families, 75 per cent were following their parents in 1963, while in 2025 only 26 per cent were doing so.

The strength of party identification has weakened too. In 1964 a total of 36 per cent of those identifying with a party said they were very strongly attached, and 43 per cent felt fairly strongly attached. The remaining fifth described their identification as not very strong. The introduction of three-party competition was accompanied by a reduction of strong identifiers to 29 per cent in 1974 and 20 per cent in 1983. The strength of identification as well as the number of people identifying with a party continues to shrink. In 2024 only 13 per cent of respondents felt very strongly about their party identification.

At a time when voters are becoming increasingly detached from parties, the BES question overstates the extent to which people have a party identification because it does not offer respondents the option of saying they don't identify with a party. After naming the Conservative, Labour and Liberal Democrat Parties it adds only the vague alternative 'or what'. A survey by John Bartle (2001) asked one group the standard BES question and the other group: *Many people think of themselves as being Conservative, Labour, Liberal Democrat (or Nationalist), even if they don't always support that party. How about you? Generally speaking, do you think of yourself as Conservative, Labour, Liberal Democrat (or Nationalist), or don't you think of yourself as any of these?* A quarter of a century ago 32 per cent said they had no party identification. This was much more than the 12 per cent saying they had no party identification when asked the standard BES question. This suggests that today a majority of Britons would not think of themselves as having a party identification.

People change their minds between elections

Once a new Parliament meets, an electoral cycle begins in which a government has five years during which its actions are very much discussed in the media and individuals discuss informally with friends and people at work. The government of the day faces a variety of problems, some offering popular decisions, such as raising social benefits, while others involve unpopular measures, such as raising taxes. The strategic aim of government is to be popular when it most counts, at the time of a general election. During the life of a parliament, voters can change their minds about who should govern. In what William Nordhaus (1975) has called the political business cycle, it is rational for a newly elected government to take unpopular decisions early in its term of office in hopes that its actions will be offset subsequently by decisions that will encourage re-election.

Politicians have three partisan sources of information about their standing with the electorate: exchanges of opinion with their fellow MPs, discussions with supporters in their constituency and opinions voiced on the leader-pages of the papers they read. There is also a readily available source: surveys of public opinion conducted by the standards of the British Polling Council. Less frequently available are by-election results that show the party that won the seat at the previous general election has lost thousands of votes and sometimes the seat itself.

Sample surveys of public opinion

The frequent publication of surveys informs politicians whether the voters who put them in office are wavering in their support. MPs can look to the polls for an indication of the risk they face of losing their seat at the next election, and anxious MPs can then press their leader to do something to stave off this happening. Because polls are about a hypothetical event – voting if an election were held today – such surveys give feedback that party strategists can take into account in their continuous campaign for re-election (see Butler and Butler, 2011: 300–312; Pack, 2025).

In the era of the two-party system, there was limited wavering in support for the government during the life of a parliament. Between the 1951 and 1955 elections, notwithstanding a change in a prime minister from Winston Churchill to Anthony Eden, there was only a seven-point difference between the high and the low in support for the Conservative government. Support for the government of Harold Wilson varied only 9 percentage points in his short first term in office beginning in 1964. However, during his second term monthly popularity ranged between a high of 53 per cent and a low of 28 per cent when the economy got into trouble. In the seven parliaments of the two-party system, the spread between the high and low of the governing party's monthly poll support averaged 14 percentage points.

The introduction of a party system with hybrid competition in 1974 led to greater volatility in the monthly poll support of governing parties by enabling governing party supporters to defect to the Liberal Democrats, a halfway house ideologically. This increased the distance between the high and low of support for each governing party during a parliament. When Margaret Thatcher was prime minister, the gap between the high and low points for the Conservatives was 23 percentage points. When Tony Blair was prime minister, this gap was as high as 28 percentage points. In the next three parliaments those saying they would vote for the Conservative governments fluctuated an average of 23 percentage points. This fell to 17 per cent in June 2019.

In the 2019–24 Parliament the proportion expressing a Conservative voting intention fluctuated by a record 36 percentage points. It reached a high of 55 per cent four months after Boris Johnson led the government to victory in the 'Get Brexit done' election. Johnson's personal behaviour then pushed voter support down to 19 per cent shortly before he resigned as prime minister to avoid censure for contempt of Parliament. Instead of benefiting from a political business cycle, Rishi Sunak found himself in a loop of doom. From when he took office to the 2024 election campaign, Conservative support fluctuated narrowly between 21 per cent and 25 per cent. Poll satisfaction with Keir Starmer's government fell to a low of 19 per cent in autumn 2025, a level 15 percentage points below its relatively high a month after the election (see Appendix Table 3).

By-elections

The outcome of a by-election presents real evidence of whether voters have changed their minds since a general election. When the result is a defeat for the defending party, the entry of the winner into the House of Commons confronts MPs with a reminder of the possibility that they may lose their own seat at the next election.

By-elections are by definition unrepresentative of the electorate as a whole. Each reflects voters in only one of Parliament's 650 constituencies. A multiplicity of conditions can cause a by-election by the sitting MP vacating their seat: death or resignation; appointment to the House of Lords; sexual misbehaviour; bankruptcy or conviction of a serious crime; or a recall petition signed by at least 10 per cent of the voters in a constituency in which the MP has been found guilty of misconduct. By-elections tend to be randomly distributed among constituencies. As the largest party by far in the House of Commons, Labour is much more vulnerable to having to defend a seat in a by-election than either the Conservatives or Reform.

A by-election offers voters a chance to protest their dissatisfaction with the government of the day. Since control of government is not at stake, voters can also favour a party that best represents their views whether or not it is a governing party. This gives Liberal Democrats, Greens and nationalists an advantage. Since the turnout of voters at a by-election is almost invariably lower than at a general election, all parties, including the winner, may have the size of their vote fall.

The most politically significant by-elections are those in which a seat changes hands. For the government, a by-election offers little benefit and significant risk. If it loses the seat, this is a public slight and demoralising for its MPs, who project the result on to their own chance of re-election. Opposition parties can gain kudos if they win a seat. Less certainly, it is an auger of a potential increase in votes at the next general election.

By-elections were held more often during the period of two-party competition, an average of 10 a year. Between 1945 and 1966 the government of the day lost an average of only one seat a year. The pattern then changed abruptly. In the 1966–70 Parliament the average number of by-elections a year was halved but the Labour government set the record for the most by-elections lost in a Parliament, 15. In the nine by-elections held during the Conservative government elected in 1970, the Liberals won five, a harbinger of the party's breakthrough at the February 1974 general election (see Butler and Butler, 2011: 284ff; Cracknell, 2022).

Three-party competition increased pressure on the governing party to stop creating by-elections by appointing MPs to the Lords and to encourage MPs in declining health not to retire. The number of by-elections fell to four a year, and government defeats fell too during the 18 years of Conservative government from 1979. The Liberal Democrats and the Scottish National Party were the principal beneficiaries of the Conservative government's by-election defeats.

The number of by-elections dropped to a record low during the 1997–2010 Labour government, averaging only 2.8 per year. Labour lost six seats. During the two Conservative governments struggling with Brexit from 2015 to 2019 there were 18 by-elections, but only three seats changed hands, the lowest turnover in the postwar era. The number of by-elections in the 2019–24 Parliament, 23, was no different from preceding decades but the results were. Early in the Parliament the Johnson government won Hartlepool, which Labour had held since the constituency was created in 1974. The Conservatives lost 11 seats; two-thirds of their defeats were suffered in the 12 months leading up to the 2024 general election.

Even if a by-election does not result in a seat changing hands, it does show whether voters are wavering from their general election choice. The most common form of wavering is not voting. By-election turnout is as much as one-third lower than at a general election. In the 2019 Parliament, turnout averaged only 37.1 per cent. Thus, the result of a single by-election not only fails to represent the tens of millions of voters who do not live in the constituency; it also does not represent the majority of voters who do live there.

Voters make choices during an election campaign

When a general election is called, the electorate is divided into those who have already made up their minds and those who are uncertain how they will vote. Even if the undecided are in a minority, they tend to be sufficient in number to decide the outcome in a first-past-the-post electoral system. Late deciders tend to be more numerous among women and younger voters (Willocq, 2019).

Before the 1992 election was called, an Ipsos MORI survey found that 63 per cent of voters reported they had already decided which party they would vote for. Among the 37 per cent who were undecided, 21 per cent made up their minds during the last week of the campaign. By 2010 the proportion saying they had decided in the final week of the campaign had risen to 26 per cent while the number who had made up their mind about voting before the campaign began had dropped by 6 percentage points. An alternative way to assess vote commitment when a general election is called is to ask the degree of certainty that people have about their party preference. When YouGov did this at the start of the 2024 general election campaign, 43 per cent said they had definitely made up their mind about how they would vote while almost one-third did not know how they would vote,

Left–right ideology and multi-dimensional values

Identifying parties in ideological terms such as left and right does not require ordinary people to have a detailed knowledge of parties in order to perceive them as they have historically seen themselves. However, left–right characteristics are not the only political values that individuals may hold. Since the number of clusters that can be formed is not limited to a single dimension, different value dimensions are especially likely to occur when there is competition between six parties. The extent to which people hold a particular set of values is an empirical question.

Divisions left, right and then some

The Labour and Conservative Parties have long been characterised as representing left-wing and right-wing ideologies (Beer, 1965). The Labour Party has been associated with the socio-economic left, given its historic advocacy of socialist principles and its working-class electoral base. The Conservatives have historically been associated with conserving traditional forms of authority based on social standing and wealth. This ideological dichotomy is consistent with the two-party system. However, it has been challenged by the leaders of both parties. Margaret Thatcher promoted a free-market economic ideology and individual responsibility for welfare more akin to historic liberal values. In the 1980s the Social Democratic Party briefly advanced a combination of right-wing economic policies and social policies of the left. Tony Blair offered a New Labour outlook that combined elements of both left and right, as in the dictum 'Tough on crime, tough on the causes of crime'.

Many political surveys ask voters how they place themselves on a one-dimensional 11-point left–right scale. The British Electoral Study describes the zero end as left and point ten as right; it leaves all the intermediate points unlabelled. The great majority of respondents place themselves at one of the unmarked alternatives. The interpretation of the nine unlabelled points is ambiguous. Literally, they can be described as less left or less right or closer to the centre than to an explicit political ideology.

YouGov offers respondents a clearly labelled set of alternatives. *Some people talk about 'left', 'right' and 'centre' to describe parties and politicians. With this in mind, where would you place parties? yourself?* A choice of seven alternatives is offered, each clearly labelled for interpretation: *very left-wing, fairly left-wing, slightly left of centre, centre, slightly right of centre, fairly right-wing* and *very right-wing.* Those who answer don't know are recorded separately (Difford, 2025). For convenience in measuring the distance between parties, their placement is converted into an equal-interval scale running from very left-wing (minus 100) to very right-wing (plus 100).

Voters divide themselves into four almost equal categories: left, centre, right and don't know. A total of 29 per cent place themselves to the left of centre; 26 per cent right of centre; 22 per cent put themselves in the centre and an equal percentage don't know where to place themselves (Figure 3.1). Thus, 44 per cent reject placing themselves on the left or on the right. Those who did make an ideological choice divided almost equally into being slightly left or right of centre or fairly or very left or right. The evidence rejects the view that the British electorate is ideologically polarised. The distribution of voters is bell-shaped. Three-fifths of those who place themselves ideologically are either in the centre or slightly to one side or the other, while less than one-sixth are fairly or very much on the left and another sixth clearly on the right.

Voters see parties as divided into two families, left and right. In YouGov's March 2025 survey the Greens are the furthest to the left, –55; Labour is at –36; and the Liberal Democrats are at –22. In Scotland and Wales respondents placed the Scottish National Party and Plaid Cymru to the left of Labour at –42. No party is seen as close to the centre. The Conservatives are assessed at 51, halfway between the centre and very right. Reform

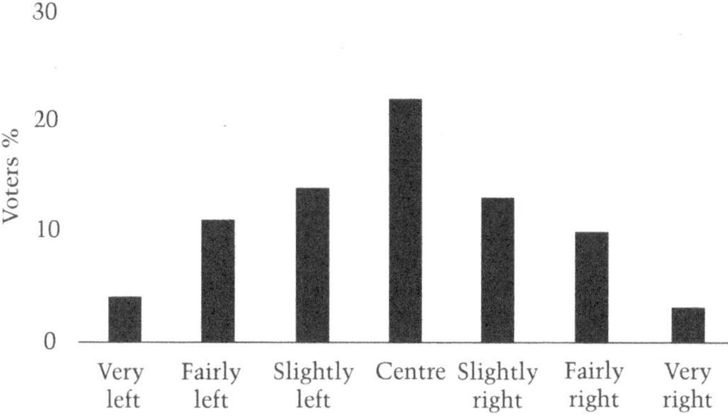

Figure 3.1 Left–right self-placement of voters
Source: YouGov survey of 1,193 respondents who gave both a left–right position and a party preference, 26 March 2025. No bar is shown for the 22 per cent of respondents who could not place themselves.

UK is seen as further to the right at 69. While the median voter is in the centre, no party is placed there. There is a gap of 73 points between the Liberal Democrats on the left and the Conservatives on the right.

The political ideology of voters is partially related to their party choice. Among those who see themselves on the left, 63 per cent favour Labour and an additional 30 per cent divide almost equally between the Greens and the Liberal Democrats. While it is arithmetically correct to note that the great majority in this group support a left-wing party, it is politically misleading, since these left-wing parties compete with each other for votes and seats in the House of Commons.

More than four-fifths of voters on the right favour the Conservatives or Reform UK as against 10 per cent favouring Labour. Among Reform UK supporters, 57 per cent placed themselves on the right; one-fifth placed themselves in the centre; and a fifth were don't knows. Similarly, among Conservative supporters, 61 per cent placed themselves on the right, a fifth took a centre position and a sixth were don't knows.

Self-consciously centrist voters have no strongly preferred party. Instead, they divide themselves among all five parties, with a tilt slightly left of centre. The median voter in this group favoured the Liberal Democrats. Support for the two governing parties divided in the ratio of four centrists favouring Labour for every three favouring the Conservatives. Reform received more support from centrists than the Greens in a survey taken before Zack Polanski began aggressively emphasising left-wing views.

Multi-dimensional values

The values of voters relate to many different political dimensions. Some are linked to conventional left–right differences, such as attitudes towards taxation and economic inequality. Others focus on non-economic concerns such as patriotism and LGBTQ rights. Individual attitudes cannot be reduced to a single dimension. Political values form a multiplicity of ideologies that may or may not link with the values of parties.

The 2023 British Social Attitudes survey asked a heterogeneous range of questions about attitudinal values. On this basis, the statistical analysis of John Curtice and Lovisa Vallgarda (2024) grouped respondents into six unequally sized groups defined by their shared values. The percentages given for each group show their share of respondents:

- *Well-Off Traditionalists* (12%). White, religious and higher-status Britons who dislike taxes and public expenditure.
- *Left-Behind Patriots* (15%). Proud of Britain's past more than its present, against diversity policies, struggle financially and disenchanted with politics.
- *Apolitical Centrists* (17%). View levels of immigration and welfare spending as about right; less comfortable financially; and have little interest in politics.
- *Middle Britons* (26%). Distribution of wealth unfair to ordinary people but do not support more government taxing and spending, and favour tough policies on crime.
- *Soft-Left Liberals* (14%). Well-educated professionals, centrist on economics and liberal on issues such as civil rights and immigration.
- *Woke Progressives* (16%). Left wing on economic issues, relatively young and urban, anti-racist and pro-women's and LGBTQ rights.

The number of value divisions, six, is closer to today's disrupted party system than it is to the two-party or three-party systems that preceded it. In so far as values influence voting, then people in each cluster ought to vote for the same parties within a family of left-wing parties (Labour, Green and Liberal Democrat) or of right-wing parties (Conservatives and Reform UK). However, Curtice and Vallgarda (2024) find only limited support for the hypothesis that people with shared values share the same party preferences.

Three different value groups with 42 per cent of the electorate show a strong correlation with a preference for a party family. Unsurprisingly, among Woke Progressives 93 per cent favoured the Labour–Liberal Democrat–Green family and 87 per cent of Soft-Left Liberals were equally united in favouring the left family. On the other hand, among Well-Off Traditionalists four-fifths favoured the Conservative–Reform family.

In three clusters with 58 per cent of the electorate, voters divide their support across two families and five parties. Among Middle Britons and Left-Behind Patriots the more favoured family receives only 52 per cent of the vote. The family of right-wing parties collectively receives 59 per cent of votes cast by Apolitical Centrists while 36 per cent of that group cast their votes for parties of the left.

Voters' left–right position and values can help decide which family of parties they won't vote for. However, they leaves open which of the two or three parties within their family they choose to vote for. When Britons cast their vote, they are not confronted with a choice between left–right families. They make a single choice from among up to half a dozen party candidates.

Open-minded voters

Parties prefer getting their votes from long-term supporters who back them without question through thick and thin because of the influence of family and class.

These require much less effort to hold than open-minded voters who can give them their vote today and be gone well before the next election. However, their pool of long-term supporters is insufficient to keep a party's vote stable, and it contracts during the life of a parliament. They need a continuous flow of new supporters to replace those they have lost through death, emigration or political disappointment. Replacements can come from a mixture of sources: youthful first-time voters, former supporters who did not vote at the previous election or open-minded voters attracted by a party's fresh appeal.

When an election is held, voters have the choice between voting for the same party as before or supporting a different party. Being a stable voter is the simpler option. However, as class and party identification have eroded as influences, voting the same as before is no longer pre-determined. More and more voters have become open-minded. Open-minded voters make a fresh assessment of their party choice based on their perception of how parties have performed and what issues have become more significant or less significant since the last election. Even if a concern with the economy is constant, the challenge it presents can shift from being about economic growth to being about the cost of living and inflation.

Switching between the Conservative and Labour Parties has a double effect, for it adds a vote to one governing party and takes a vote from the other. However, direct switching between governing parties is very limited. The Liberal Democrats have long offered a halfway house for voters wanting to withdraw their support from a governing party. Moving to the Lib Dems from Labour or the Conservatives subtracts a vote from one governing party without adding it to the other. Today a voter has a choice of moving to one of three non-governing parties in England and four in Scotland and Wales.

Reasons for choice

When making a party choice, open-minded voters can decide according to an ad hoc assessment of how parties are currently performing, whereas the reasons that lead committed partisans to vote the same are unchanging from one election to the next. However, even if open-minded voters endorse the same party, they may do so for different reasons, such as how it managed the economy or if they like its immigration policy.

When respondents were asked by YouGov to choose the most important reasons for deciding how to vote from a list of 11 different alternatives, they divided into three virtually equal groups (Table 3.2). While only 3 per cent said they had always voted for the same party, three reasons were endorsed that indicated a long-term stable commitment. Chief among these reasons was the view that the party they supported shared their values and that it stood up for people like themselves. A few mentioned it was the party of people in their community.

Most respondents gave reasons based on ad hoc current conditions, divided almost equally between those who

Table 3.2 Reasons for deciding how to vote (%)

Long-term stable commitment (32)	
Shares my values	20
Stands up for people like me	8
Always supported it	3
Most people in my community support	1
Positive ad hoc reasons (33)	
Best for my most important policy	21
Its policies helpful to me, my family	7
Has the best leader	3
Like local MP, candidate	2
Negative ad hoc reasons (32)	
Better than alternatives	21
Stop another party winning	6
Other, don't know	5

Source: YouGov survey of 4,006 respondents, 2–5 June 2025.

were casting a positive vote *for* a party and those casting a negative vote *against* a party. The most common positive reasons for choosing a party were that it appeared best able to deal with whatever the voter thought important and that it would help their family. New parties may gain support by raising a hitherto neglected issue, such as the pro-environment Green Party or Reform UK, which has flourished by making an issue of immigration. Notwithstanding the media attention given political personalities, only 5 per cent said they were voting primarily to support a party leader or a constituency candidate.

A third of respondents gave ad hoc negative reasons, indicating little or no attachment to the party they were currently supporting. It was simply seen as better than the alternatives. Tactical voting to keep another party from winning, such as a failed party of government, motivates only a small fraction of the electorate. This reflects the conditions for tactical voting being evident only in a limited fraction of constituencies. Moreover, the governing party viewed as failed at the next general election will be different from the failed party at the last election.

Parties differ in number of long-term and open-minded supporters

From one election to the next, British parties differ greatly in their capacity to attract long-term and short-term voters. The Labour Party won the 2024 general election because it held those who had supported it under Jeremy Corbyn at the previous election and won additional support from other parties. Almost half of the open-minded voters that Labour recruited were disaffected Conservatives, and two-fifths were former Liberal Democrats. Moreover, Labour gained almost an eighth of its 2024 vote from 18- to 24-year-olds who were too young to vote at the previous general election. Of the 2019 voters who drifted away, a big majority went to other parties in the left-wing family; only one-sixth of Labour defectors went to Reform UK or the Conservatives in 2024. The net effect of all these changes was a 1.6 percentage point increase in Labour's share of the national vote. Notwithstanding this relative boost, Labour lost half a million votes from its 2019 total vote. It was the first-past-the-post electoral system rather than a swell in popular support in the electorate that produced Labour's massive parliamentary majority.

Because the Conservatives won the most votes in the 2019 election, they were the most vulnerable to losing support in 2024. The failings of the Tory government resulted in the party losing 47 per cent of its former voters, a sum equivalent to one-fifth of all who voted in the 2024 election. Almost three-fifths of its defectors went to its ideologically closest rival, Reform UK. Demographic turnover added to the contraction in the Conservative vote, since its 8 per cent of the under-25 vote fell well short of replacing its loss of voters over 70, where the party has been strongest. The Conservatives also lost one-quarter of their former supporters in the opposite ideological direction, to Labour, the Liberal Democrats and the Greens.

As a halfway house between the two governing parties, the Liberal Democrats experienced a high level of churn among their voters. They were able to hold on to only half their 2019 supporters. This was because they campaigned on a platform of turning the Tories out of office. Since Labour was better placed to win many more seats from the Tories, the Liberal Democrats lost almost one-third of their former supporters to Labour. The Liberal Democrats gained a similar number of defectors from the Conservatives and from Labour. These gains tended to be concentrated in constituencies in which the party offered the best choice for unseating a Conservative MP. Thus, with little change in their share of the national vote, the Liberal Democrats increased their representation in the House of Commons more than six times (Griffiths, Green and Fieldhouse, 2024).

The Green vote more than doubled at the 2024 election. Gains from former Labour voters contributed about three-quarters of the 4-percentage-point increase in the Greens' vote. The Greens lost one-quarter of their former voters to Labour and 14 per cent to the Liberal Democrats. However, these losses were small in absolute terms because the Greens had gained only 2.7 per cent of the national vote in 2019.

Since Reform UK did not fight the 2019 election, it depended on attracting voters from other parties who favoured immigration, which was its key issue. The Conservatives were a doubly attractive source to take from. Not only were their voters close to Reform on major issues but also Tory government shortcomings, including the handling of immigration, had reduced the attachment of its voters. Thus, the 25 per cent of Conservatives who defected accounted for three-quarters of Reform's 14.3 per cent share of the national vote. Defectors to Reform from other parties were few and scattered.

Multi-party voters

In their political lifetime, a large portion of Britons are multi-party voters, that is, they cast their vote for different parties in the many elections in which they have participated. The actions of politicians in organising new parties have more than doubled the number of parties and candidates offered voters. Of the record number of 6.8 million who voted Liberal Democrat in 2010, more than two-thirds changed their preference at the following election. Similarly, the great majority of the 1.9 million who voted for the Greens in 2024 are multi-party voters since the party had only recently started contesting seats nationwide. Virtually the whole of the 4.1 million who voted for Reform in 2024 are multi-party voters, since the party had not contested any previous election.

National surveys of voters provide a fuller picture of multi-party voters. They take into account the gross change of voters in all directions, movements that are lost sight of in calculating the net change in a party's vote from national election statistics. Surveys such as the British Election Study and YouGov, which ask people how they have voted at a previous election as well as currently, provide evidence of people becoming multi-party voters in the short term.

In 1966 only one-eighth of BES respondents reported switching their vote. The proportion changing parties rose to one in four by the 1992 election. In 2010 almost one in three were multi-party voters between two elections. There was a peak in switching in 2015, when 42 per cent reported changing the party they endorsed from the previous election (Andersen, 2019). An account of individuals' lifetime voting pattern, if not affected by recall bias, would show a clear majority of electors being multi-party voters.

To describe multi-party voters as floating voters is to misunderstand the conditions that make people change how they vote from time to time. They may have consistent views on political issues that lead them to change their party choice if their initially preferred party changes its policies or fails to deliver what it has pledged when it is in government. When national conditions change, individuals can change their minds about the importance of issues such as inflation or unemployment. They may change their vote as their personal circumstances change, for example having children in school or retiring from work to live from a pension. To stigmatise voters as unstable because they are open-minded about changing parties assumes that Britons should persist in voting for the same party from one decade to another whatever its performance rather than holding parties accountable for their performance between one parliament and the next.

Citations

Abrams, Mark and Rose, Richard, 1960. *Must Labour Lose?* Harmondsworth: Penguin Books.

Andersen, Peter, 2019. 'How many voters really switch parties in British elections?' https://news.liverpool.ac.uk/2019/11/27/how-many-voters-really-switch-parties-in-british-elections-what-the-evidence-tells-us/. Accessed 21 December 2025.

Bartle, John, 2001. *The Measurement of Party Identification in the United Kingdom: Technical Details and Codebook*. Colchester: UK Data Service.

Beer, Samuel H., 1965. *Modern British Politics*. London: Faber and Faber.

Butler, David and Butler, Gareth, 2011. *British Political Facts*. London: Palgrave Macmillan, 10th edition.

Butler, David and Stokes, Donald, 1969 (1st edition) and 1974 (2nd edition). *Political Change in Britain*. London: Macmillan.

Campbell, Angus, Converse, P. E., Miller, W. E. and Stokes, D. E., 1960. *The American Voter*. New York: John Wiley.

Clarke, Harold D. and Stewart, Marianne C., 1998. 'The decline of parties in the minds of citizens'. In Nelson Polsby, ed., *Annual Review of Political Science*. Palo Alto: Annual Reviews.

Cracknell, Richard, 2022. *By-elections*. London: House of Commons Library Briefing Papers.

Curtice, John and Vallgarda, Lovisa Moller, 2024. *How the Value Divide Is Challenging Britain's Two-Party System*. London: National Centre for Social Research.

Difford, Dylan, 2025. 'Where do Britons see politicians, parties and themselves on the left-right spectrum?' London: YouGov, https://yougov.co.uk/politics/articles/52080-where-do-britons-see-politicians-parties-and-themselves-on-the-left-right-spectrum. Accessed 21 December 2025.

Gallup, 1976. 'Voting behaviour in Britain, 1945–1974'. In R. Rose, ed., *Studies in British Politics*. London: Macmillan, 3rd edition.

Goodwin, Matthew and Milazzo, Caitlin, 2017. 'Taking back control? Investigating the role of immigration in the 2016 vote for Brexit', *British Journal of Politics and International Relations*, 19, 3, 450–464.

Griffiths, James D., Green, Jane and Fieldhouse, Ed, 2024. 'The Liberal Democrats in 2024: efficiency and tactical voting'. Manchester: British Election Study.

Hawkins, Oliver and Loft, Philip, 2020. *General Election 2019: Results and Analysis*. London: House of Commons Library Briefing paper, 2nd edition.

McKenzie, Robert T. and Silver, Allan, 1968. *Angels in Marble*. London: Heinemann.

Nordhaus, William D., 1975. 'The political business cycle', *Review of Economic Studies*, 42, 2, 169–190.

Norris, Pippa, 1997. *Electoral Change since 1945*. Oxford: Blackwell.

Pack, Mark, 2025. 'The week in polls', theweekinpolls@substack.com. Accessed 21 December 2025.

Pulzer, Peter, 1967. *Political Representation and Elections in Britain*. London: Allen & Unwin.

Rose, Richard, 1968. 'Class and party divisions: Britain as a test case', *Sociology*, 2, 2, 129–162.

Rose, Richard and McAllister, Ian, 1986. *Voters Begin to Choose: From Closed-Class to Open Elections in Britain*. London: Sage Publications.

Willocq, Simon, 2019. 'Explaining time of vote decision', *Policy Studies Review*, 17, 1, 53–64.

YouGov, 2022. 'Britons are split on whether they would support compulsory voting', https://ygo-assets-websites-editorial-emea.yougov.net/documents/YouGov_-_Compulsory_Voting_Results.pdf. Accessed 21 December 2025.

4
2024: The great disruption

The 2024 general election disrupted the classic British system of party competition. Non-governing parties collectively won the largest share of the popular vote, 42.6 per cent, an increase of more than 18 percentage points from the previous election. This unprecedented total was more than the vote of the winning party in 11 general elections since 1974. In all, 303 seats changed hands, the greatest number since the 1930s. Eleven non-governing parties held at least one seat in the House of Commons. Because non-governing parties are a category rather than a single party, collectively they add five new dimensions to party competition: the environment, Europe, independence from Westminster, immigration and religion. However, because they are divided, no party in the group was relevant to Labour taking control of government with a big majority.

The governing parties set records for poor performance. Labour won government with the lowest share of the national vote, 33.7 per cent, of any majority government since the introduction of universal suffrage. Its vote was actually 6 percentage points lower than when it lost the

2017 election under Jeremy Corbyn. Labour owed its victory to the first-past-the-post electoral system rather than to the electoral appeal of Keir Starmer's revamped Labour Party. It won 63 per cent of seats, only a little short of double its percentage of the vote. If Labour had benefited to the same extent of over-representation as enjoyed by the Conservatives in 2019, it would have fallen well short of a parliamentary majority with only 282 seats. The Conservative Party recorded the worst electoral defeat in its history, winning only 23.7 per cent of the vote and 121 seats. Thus, the combined vote for the two governing parties, Labour and the Conservatives, was the lowest on record.

At the constituency level there are up to six parties for voters to choose from in more than six hundred constituencies. In addition to Labour and the Conservatives, there are the Liberal Democrats, Reform UK, the Greens, the SNP or Plaid Cymru, and, in constituencies with a high proportion of Muslim voters, there can be pro-Palestine candidates. Voters must first make a meta-choice: whether to vote for a governing party or a party that represents a distinctive political outlook but has no chance of governing. If they choose the former, there is then a choice of which governing party to vote for or against. If they choose to vote against the party currently in control of government, there is then a need to choose between parties representing a multiplicity of competing policy dimensions.

Open-minded voters did more than waver: they switched between parties in great numbers. In 2024 the volatility in the party vote almost doubled from the 2019 election. The total ups and downs in party shares of the vote was 42 per cent, the highest level of volatility since the disruption in three-party competition at the 1931 economic-crisis election. The Conservative Party's collapse was the most important cause of volatility. Its support fell by seven million votes and its share of the national vote fell by 19.9 percentage points. The Reform UK party was the second-biggest cause of volatility. Its vote went up by 3.4 million and its share of the national vote rose by more than 12 percentage points by comparison with the performance of the UK Independence Party at the previous election. The Green Party was the third significant contributor to volatility; its share of the national vote went up 4 percentage points and its national vote was up by one million.

This chapter shows how disruption is making competition between six parties the norm. Nationally, the disproportional first-past-the-post electoral system still favours two parties alternating in control of government. However, at the constituency level it favours the two parties finishing first or second. The same two governing parties are no longer the two front-runners in almost every constituency. Instead, in a majority of constituencies one and sometimes both front-runners are non-governing parties. The two front-running parties differ from place to place. In the South-west of England, Conservatives and Liberal Democrats compete, while in the North of England it is often

Labour and Reform competing. In the London area it is usually Labour and Conservatives in first and second place, but in Scotland a Westminster party competes with the SNP. Thus, general elections are no longer general.

Six parties compete for seats

While only one party can win a constituency, election law set no limit on the number of candidates that can appear on a constituency ballot. The chief requirements are filing a nomination form signed by ten constituents and depositing £500 returnable if the candidate wins at least 5 per cent of the constituency vote. A candidate can be identified on the ballot with a party registered with the Electoral Commission. The name of each party's leader appears on the ballot only in the constituency they are contesting.

The system of electoral competition places two major obstacles in the way of politicians aspiring to launch a national party. First of all, a British party must recruit up to six hundred constituency candidates in order to compete nationwide for votes. Secondly, a party must raise £300,000 or more to meet the collective cost of deposits. In an era of campaigning by mass media and social media, an organisation to canvass voters on the ground is not necessary. However, a centralised party headquarters needs local knowledge to vet six-hundred-plus candidates effectively in order to make sure they have nothing embarrassing on record in their past or current life.

Candidates multiply

In the two-party system, wherever one looked on the map the pattern was the same: Labour and Conservative candidates competed to become the constituency's MP. At the height of this system in 1951 the two governing parties finished first or second in all but a handful of constituencies. The number of candidates per constituency, averaging 2.2, was the lowest in the post-1945 period and the 142 candidates of other parties or independents were very much also-rans. In 1970 the Conservative and Labour Parties came first and second in 93.0 per cent of British constituencies.

The three-party system came into being when the Liberals began to nominate candidates to fight the great majority of seats. In February 1974, the party nominated 517 candidates, their highest number since 1906, and there were 372 other candidates. For the first time the total number of candidates went over two thousand and the average number rose to 3.3 per constituency. Thus, the proportion of constituencies in which the Conservatives and Labour were the two dominant parties fell to 70 per cent. The average number of candidates per constituency reached four at the 1992 election and five in 1997. For the first time, in the 2010 election an average of six candidates contested each constituency. However, in 2019 the two governing parties partially recovered, and the average number of candidates per constituency dropped to 5.1. The 2024 election saw a jump upwards in the number of candidates to 4,515, the largest number on record. In Scotland and Wales, the average number of candidates was above seven, while in England it averaged just below seven candidates per constituency.

The growth in the number of parties dividing the vote in each constituency means that MPs no longer represent a majority of their voters. The peak in majority representation occurred in 1955: 593 MPs represented more than half their constituency's voters. The introduction of three-party competition has effectively lowered the standard for winning a seat. In February 1974, the Liberal Party breakthrough created a House of Commons in which 64 per cent of MPs represented a minority of their voters. This was the first time since 1832 that most MPs did not represent a majority of their voters.

The number of MPs elected with less than half the vote has gone up and down since then. At the 2024 election 554 MPs were elected by less than half the vote and ten with 30 per cent of the vote or less. In Norfolk South West, the Labour candidate won the seat from former prime minister Liz Truss with 26.7 per cent of the vote. Only one Conservative MP won more than 50 per cent of their constituency vote. The 50 per cent plus club also included 70 Labour MPs, 18 Liberal Democrats and two Green MPs.

Holborn & St. Pancras, the London constituency of the prime minister, Keir Starmer, illustrates how the increase in candidates is disrupting party competition (Table 4.1). At the 2019 election seven parties contested the seat but only three saved their deposits and Starmer won almost two-thirds of the vote. In 2024 there were 12 candidates contesting the seat and six saved their

Table 4.1 Disruption in Keir Starmer's constituency, Holborn & St Pancras (%)

	2019	2024	Change
Labour	64.5	48.90	−17.4
Left-wing independent	0.0	18.90	18.9
Green	4.0	10.40	6.4
Brexit/Reform	1.9	6.10	4.2
Liberal Democrats	12.3	5.80	−6.5
Conservative	15.2	7.20	−8.0
Independent (Wais Islam)	0.0	1.60	1.6
Monster Raving Loony	0.0	0.40	0.4
UKIP	0.3	0.20	−0.1
Socialist Equality	0.1	0.20	0.1
Independent (Senthil Kumar)	0.0	0.10	0.1
Give Me Back Elmo	0.0	0.03	0.3

Note: Results adjusted to take into account minor boundary changes in the constituency after 2019.
Source: https://members.parliament.uk/constituency/4105/election/422

deposits. Starmer's vote dropped by around one-quarter, resulting in him representing a minority of voters. A left-wing independent candidate, Andrew Feinstein, who had not contested the seat previously, came second. Green and Reform candidates saved their deposits too.

Given the fixed size of the House of Commons, an increase in the number of candidates means an increase in the number of losers. In the 625 constituencies contested at the 1951 election, there were only 126 losers above the democratic minimum of one loser per constituency. The total number of losing candidates rose above one thousand for the first time in 1964. The lowering of the vote required to save a deposit reduced the cost of losing. By 1992 the number of losing candidates rose above two thousand, and it went above three thousand in 1997. At the 2024 general election, 3,865 candidates were losers. Reform UK and the Greens were the leading losers; each party lost more than six hundred seats. However, not all losers are politically irrelevant.

Relevant parties increase

The sorting of British parties into major or minor categories is conventionally determined by whether a party alternates in and out of government. All other parties, however many millions of votes they gain, are considered minor parties.

The relevance of non-governing parties to government depends on the number of seats it has and the seats of the largest party in the Commons. When the governing party has a small majority or loses it as a result of by-election defeats and defections, a few MPs can make a big impact. The Labour government of Jim Callaghan lost a no-confidence motion by one vote in 1979. By contrast, when the Liberal Democrats gained 72 MPs in 2024, more than any third party in a century, they were irrelevant to government, because Labour won an overwhelming Commons majority.

At the constituency level, non-governing parties can be relevant in three different ways. By splitting the majority of a constituency's vote up to six different ways, they turn its MP into the representative of a minority of its voters. Secondly, a non-governing party can undermine a governing party's MP by taking votes from it. In 137 of the seats the Conservatives lost to Labour in 2024, the combined Conservative and Reform share of the vote was bigger than that of Labour (Prosser, 2024). A third form of relevance comes from tactical voting, as non-governing voters switch to a second-place candidate in order to oust an incumbent. In 2024 tactical voting helped second-place Liberal Democrats make a big breakthrough as supporters of an also-ran Labour candidate voted Liberal Democrat to protest against the government by ousting a Conservative MP.

As a rule of thumb, constituency candidates can be described as relevant if they win enough votes to save their deposit. When the standard for saving a deposit was 12.5 per cent of the constituency vote, non-governing candidates were usually irrelevant because they did not contest many constituencies. However, the disillusionment of the electorate with the two governing parties at the February 1974 election enabled the Liberal Democrats not only to increase the number of their candidates by more than half but also to save 96 per cent of their deposits. By 1979, tactical voting to turn the Labour government out squeezed the Liberal Democrats. Fewer than half their candidates saved their deposit.

While winning 5 per cent of the vote to save a deposit is inadequate to win a seat, it is enough to be relevant in a constituency contest if most of that vote is taken from a front-running Labour or Conservative candidate. Lowering the standard for saving a deposit has had the predictable effect of encouraging more candidates to stand. Between 1987 and 2024 the total number of candidates has almost doubled, along with the number of both relevant and irrelevant candidates. Fluctuations in deposits saved tend to reflect political circumstances. In 2010 no Liberal Democrat candidate lost their deposit, but at the 2015 election the unpopularity of the party joining a Conservative-led coalition resulted in 342 Liberal Democrats losing their deposit.

At the 2024 election the average number of relevant candidates increased to a record high of 4.5 per constituency. All Scottish and Welsh nationalist candidates saved their deposits, and at least 95 per cent or more of Labour, Conservative and Reform UK candidates did so too. Among the Liberal Democrat candidates, 64 per cent saved their deposits, and so did 59 per cent of Green candidates. Thus, at the next general election there will be competition between up to five relevant candidates in most English constituencies and at least six relevant candidates in Scotland and Wales.

Increasingly disproportional elections

The British electoral system is disproportional by tradition and intent. When competitive elections became common in the nineteenth century, they were held in hundreds of first-past-the-post constituencies. That practice was maintained when a democratic franchise was introduced in 1918. The fact that the system usually gives a party with a plurality of the national vote an absolute majority of MPs is cited as an asset by its proponents. Giving control of government to a single party concentrates responsibility, enabling voters to hold the government of the day accountable. This contrasts with the multi-party coalition governments created by proportional representation elections. In these, accountability is unclear and the vote of some coalition partners may go up while that of other partners goes down (Rose and Mackie, 1983).

The difference between a party's share of votes and seats is a matter of degree. Most proportional election systems do not achieve 100 per cent proportionality. The greater the number of MPs elected in a proportional-representational constituency, the greater the degree of proportionality. In the Netherlands, where the 150-seat Second Chamber forms a single constituency, the party with the biggest number of representatives is within a percentage point or so of its share of the vote. A party with two-thirds of 1 per cent of the national vote will get one seat.

Where votes are cast is more important to a party than how many votes it gets nationally. A party can win 4.1 million votes by contesting 609 seats yet gain only five MPs, the experience of Reform UK in 2024. Alternatively, a party may gain only 724,000 votes yet win nine of the 57 constituencies it contests, as the Scottish National Party did in 2024. The disparity arose because the SNP fights only Scottish seats whereas Reform contests constituencies throughout Britain. Thus, in the constituencies it fought the SNP gained an average of 12,707 votes, while by contesting seats across Britain Reform gained only 6,760 constituency votes but more than five times the national vote of the SNP.

The party that wins the most votes nationally invariably gets a larger share of seats in Parliament than of the popular vote, while the party finishing second may gain more or fewer seats than its vote share, depending on the circumstances of the election. Parties that finish third or lower normally win a smaller proportion of MPs than of votes.

During the period of the two-party system the difference between the parties' share of the vote and seats was as low as 6 per cent in 1951. By 1970 the degree of disproportionality in the system had risen to 17 per cent. This was not due to the leading party gaining a big advantage. The increase was due to more non-governing parties contesting seats. The establishment of a three-party system in the February 1974 election more than doubled disproportionality to 38 per cent, due to the Liberal Party winning 2 per cent of MPs but 19 per cent of the popular vote. In the 2019 election disproportionality was 26 per cent with the Conservative government the big beneficiary. The Liberal Democrats were the big loser, as their share of seats was one-sixth that of their share of votes.

The disruption of the party system in 2024 pushed disproportionality to a new height; the sum of over- and under-representation in seats was 59 percentage points. The Labour Party won a massive majority of seats with a historic minimum of the national vote. Labour's share of MPs was almost double its share of the popular vote. In a perfectly proportional electoral system Labour would have won 219 seats rather than returning 411 MPs. In a reversal of past performance, there was a difference of only 1.2 per cent between Liberal Democrats' share of votes and of seats, because it concentrated campaign efforts on seats it had a chance of winning. It thus suffered less from disproportionality than the Conservatives and the Greens. Reform UK was the big loser. Its 14.5 per cent share of the national vote won it only five seats, compared to the 94 seats it would have won under a completely proportional electoral system. Labour and Conservative strategists have seen this inequality as a good argument for first-past-the-post elections.

Non-governing parties add new dimensions

Collectively, non-governing parties are a single force subtracting from the votes won by the two governing parties. The party winning control of government had always won more votes than the total taken by non-governing parties until the 2024 general election. At that election the combined vote for non-governing parties was 42.6 per cent, almost 9 percentage points more than the vote for the Labour government (Table 4.2).

Non-governing parties are a fluid category. At the 2024 election Reform UK was a non-governing party. At the next general election it will be a potential governing party if it maintains its strong standing in the polls. At the 2024 election the five non-governing parties varied in their share of the national vote by more than 13 percentage points between Reform UK and Plaid Cymru. Their strength in the House of Commons varied greatly too from 72 Liberal Democrat MPs to four Plaid Cymru and four Green MPs. They also differed in where

Table 4.2 Non-governing parties winning most votes in 2024 election

	Votes (%)	Seats (%)	MPs
Non-governing parties	42.6	18.2	118
Reform	14.3	0.8	5
Liberal Democrat	12.2	11.0	72
Greens	6.7	0.6	4
SNP	2.5	1.4	9
Plaid Cymru	0.7	0.6	4
N. Ireland parties	2.7	2.7	18
Others	3.6	1.0	6
Labour	33.7	63.2	411
Conservatives	23.7	18.6	121

Source: Calculated by the author.

they contest seats. Three parties – Reform, the Liberal Democrats and the Greens – compete throughout Britain, the SNP and Plaid Cymru compete only in a limited number of British seats, and six parties compete for Northern Ireland's 18 seats. Unusually, in 2024 four Muslim candidates, each fighting as an independent, won their constituency contest. Among all the parties that failed to win any seats, the Workers Party of Britain, led by former Labour MP George Galloway, won the most votes, 210,000 (see chapter 8).

For tactical reasons, the two governing parties use negative terms to characterise their opponents. For example, the Scottish National Party is described as wanting to break up Great Britain. This may sound menacing in England but was endorsed by 45 per cent of Scottish voters at the 2014 referendum on Scottish independence. Reform UK is labelled an extremist party because it wants to reduce immigration substantially, while Reform wins votes because there are many voters for whom reducing immigration is an important issue that governing parties have failed to address successfully.

Non-governing parties are winning votes by promoting aims that differ from the traditional left–right economic dimension on which governing parties have long competed. Thus, they add five dimensions to the choices offered voters: immigration, protecting the environment, national independence, Europe and Muslim solidarity. Some aims involve differences of degree enabling governing parties to compete by offering incremental change, for example protecting the environment. But others are uncompromising, such as rejoining the European Union or independence from Westminster.

Nigel Farage originally achieved an impact on the two-party system by forming the United Kingdom Independence Party to campaign for withdrawal from the European Union. Once this was accomplished, he created Reform UK with reducing legal and illegal immigration its leading policy. This was a major issue in the minds of voters (see Table 5.1), but one that both the Labour and Conservative Parties have tried to avoid. More than that, Reform UK has framed its position as a party that offers voters a chance to protest against what it calls the 'uniparty' actions of successive Conservative and Labour governments. Its 2024 election manifesto for the most part was an amalgam of policies that could be found in one or both of the governing parties' manifestos, such as spending more money on the National Health Service and setting up a Royal Commission on social care.

The Liberal Democrats have maintained their long-standing commitment to the European Union, but instead of advocating this issue the party campaigned tactically in the 2024 election. It concentrated its campaign in about one hundred constituencies where the party had a good chance of ousting a Conservative MP forced to defend an unpopular government. Instead of emphasising what it would do if it were in government, an unlikely possibility given its status, it stressed local issues. The stunts of its leader, Ed Davey, made him appear like a friendly neighbour rather than an impressive statesman in waiting. The party won its most MPs in more than a century. By retaining their pro-EU stance, the Liberal Democrats remained distinctive from other parties.

Activist measures publicising the threat of climate change nationally and internationally have made green issues a concern of the Labour and Conservative Parties but far from their over-riding concern. The Green Party was founded in 1985 to offer voters the chance of showing it was their primary concern when they cast a ballot. At the 2024 election it became a relevant party in the competition for votes. Green candidates fought in almost every British constituency; a majority saved their deposits; and its small share of the national vote more than doubled. While both governing parties now have climate change policies, the Green Party has a unique advantage: it can campaign for climate policies without regard to the economic cost because it is not a governing party.

Nationalist parties agree in wanting to achieve independence from Westminster, but differ in how this goal may be achieved. Sinn Fein has historically endorsed the use of armed force to achieve a united Ireland. However, it has accepted the 1998 Good Friday Agreement, in which the British government offered to accept Northern Ireland leaving the United Kingdom and becoming part of a united Ireland if approved by a referendum. A variety of Ulster Unionist parties are British nationalists, that is, they give priority to remaining in the United Kingdom, a position that lacks electoral appeal in Great Britain.

The Scottish National Party's pursuit of independence has succeeded in giving it control of the devolved Scottish government since 2007 but Westminster has retained the power to decide whether an independence referendum can be held. The SNP hopes that, with demographic turnover, the failings of British government and more campaigning, a second referendum would achieve independence. Neither British governing party is willing to allow a second referendum. In the 2024 election Westminster election, the SNP stressed faults in British government as well as independence. This backfired as Labour won a majority of Scotland's seats at Westminster on the grounds that it could effectively replace an unpopular Conservative government. At the next general election the SNP hopes to do well by campaigning against a very unpopular Labour government at Westminster.

Plaid Cymru gives priority to maintaining the Welsh language. To do this requires influence on the government of Wales. The party has thus sought to increase the powers of the Welsh government in Cardiff. It can do this because the devolved government uses Welsh as well as English in official documents and the provision of public services. It can also promote the use of Welsh at all levels of education and in broadcasting. None of the parties involved in coalition governments in Cardiff is against the use of Welsh. However, fewer than one-fifth of the population of Wales say they can speak Welsh and about one-tenth are fluent Welsh-speakers. Thus, unlike the SNP, Plaid Cymru does not give priority to an independence referendum it would likely lose. Instead, it seeks more powers for the devolved Welsh government in Cardiff.

The Other category in Table 4.2 includes a mixture of 697 candidates standing under a motley variety of party labels and 459 candidates standing as independents. Of the six independent MPs, one is by convention the Speaker and the other is Jeremy Corbyn, deemed ineligible to stand for Labour but nonetheless winning his seat as an independent. Four Muslim MPs won their constituencies in the English Midlands standing as independent pro-Palestine candidates in seats that have a substantial number of Muslim voters.

Whether the measure is votes or seats, the disruption of the three-party equilibrium is evident. Any attempt to label them according to their competitive position will produce inconsistencies. For example, in 2024 Reform UK was third in its share of the vote, but tied for seventh in seats with the Democratic Unionist Party of Northern Ireland. The Greens came fifth in their share of the UK vote but dropped to eighth in their share of MPs. While collectively third parties are now the biggest party electorally, they cannot take advantage of the bias in the first-past-the-post electoral system because of the fragmentation of the non-governing vote.

General elections no longer general

For a general election to be general, the same pair of parties must be the chief choice of voters in up to 650 constituencies and agree about what divides them. Since 1945 the Labour and Conservative Parties have contested elections throughout Britain from opposing ends of the socio-economic dimension. The creation of three-party competition did not change this as the Liberal Democrats placed themselves at the centre of the left–right dimension. Thus, general elections were general. Voters had the same choice of parties and issues whatever their constituency. However, the 2024 election disrupted the governing parties' being the two leading pair of parties in constituencies. Labour and the Conservatives were the leading choices of voters in fewer than half of all constituencies.

General elections are no longer general because a variety of non-governing candidates come first or second in a majority of constituencies. Competition in each of these constituencies is now two-dimensional. Voters are offered a choice between one candidate echoing the classic American cry, 'It's the economy, stupid' and another addressing a different dimension such as 'It's immigration', 'It's climate change' or in some places 'It's independence' or 'It's Palestine'. In 118 constituencies a non-governing candidate won, and in 226 constituencies a non-governing candidate finished second.

To win seats in Parliament non-governing parties do not need to appeal to voters generally. A party needs to concentrate its efforts in a limited number of constituencies where its distinctive appeal may deliver a plurality of votes. The Scottish Nationalists and Sinn Fein have been doing this successfully for generations. In 2024 the Liberal Democrats did this too, gaining 61 target seats while increasing the number of deposits they lost elsewhere to 229. Reform UK was the biggest victim of the first-past-the-post system. Its widespread support meant that it lost only 32 deposits, yet even though winning 14 per cent of the national vote it won fewer than 1 per cent of constituencies.

Having candidates competing on up to six different dimensions gives voters a far wider range of choice of MPs to represent them than when it was confined to a pair of parties on the left and the right. The first-past-the-post electoral system introduces a meta-choice. When the party coming closest to a voter's views trails in third place or lower in a constituency, its candidate is very unlikely to win a seat in Parliament. People must then choose whether to vote for the party that best represents their views but has virtually no chance of voicing them in Parliament or voting for a second-best or lesser evil party that is sure of being in Parliament and does have a chance of taking control of government.

Constituency competition in six plus dimensions

There can only be two front-running parties in a single constituency; however, the pair of favoured parties differs greatly among the UK's 650 constituencies. Table 4.3 shows the 16 different combinations of first and second place parties in Britain in 2024, plus the ten different combinations of competition in Northern Ireland's 18 seats. The more competitive the party, the more dimensions of competition it faces. Likewise, the more it plays up to one section of the electorate, such as low-wage workers and immigrants, the more it risks losing votes to anti-immigrant parties.

Table 4.3 Multi-dimensional constituency competition in 2024

		Constituencies
Socio-economic dimension		(311)
Labour & Conservatives	219	
Labour & Socialists	5	
Conservatives & Labour	87	
Socio-economic & Europe		(86)
Lib Dems & Conservatives	84	
Lib Dems & Labour	2	
Socio-economic & immigration		(103)
Reform & Labour	92	
Reform & Conservatives	11	
Independence & socio-economic		(71)
SNP & Labour	47	
SNP & Conservatives	10	
SNP & Lib Dems	6	
Plaid Cymru & Labour	6	
Plaid Cymru & Conservatives	1	
Plaid Cymru & Lib Dems	1	

Table 4.3 (Cont.)

		Constituencies
Environment & socio-economic		(44)
Green & Labour	42	
Green & Conservatives	2	
Religion & socio-economic		
Muslim & Labour		(17)
Northern Ireland Nationalist & religion		(18)
Sinn Fein & Unionist	5	
Sinn Fein & SDLP	2	
Sinn Fein & Socialist	1	
Dem. Unionist & Alliance	3	
Dem. Unionist & Sinn Fein	2	
SDLP & Alliance	1	
Ulster Unionist & Dem Unionist	1	
Alliance & Dem. Unionist	1	
Traditional Union & Unionist	1	
Independent Unionist & Alliance	1	

Source: Author's classification of constituencies.

Labour MPs face constituency challenges on six different fronts. Little more than half their second-place constituency challengers are Conservatives and only eight are Liberal Democrats. Reform UK is second to Labour in enough constituencies to threaten its parliamentary majority. In 42 seats the Green Party is the major competitor of Labour by giving greater priority to protecting the environment than to economic growth. Muslim candidates stood as independents, but their religious appeal makes them competitive in several dozen constituencies where Muslims form a significant part of the electorate. In Scotland and Wales, nationalist MPs were the principal competitors of Labour.

Conservative candidates face major competitors in five political dimensions. The left–right dimension is the most important. However, if the Tories were to win all the 306 seats where this is the single dimension of competition, they would still fall short of winning a parliamentary majority. In the 84 constituencies where their principal opponent is a Liberal Democrat, the Conservatives can seek votes on grounds they can form a government while a Liberal Democrat vote is a wasted vote because it has no chance of governing. The Conservatives and Reform contest only 11 constituencies where they are the two front-runners. However, there are more than one hundred constituencies in which the Conservative candidate must compete with an also-ran Reform candidate for the votes needed to hold or take a seat from their principal competitor, Labour. Conservatives can fight nationalist candidates on the economic dimension, arguing that independence would be bad for the Scottish economy and oppose Green candidates by emphasising the cost of environmental policies.

Until the Brexit referendum, attitudes towards Europe were not a partisan dividing issue, because there was a consensus about membership in the European Union. Since then the Liberal Democrats have been distinctive in advocating close European Union ties. This has kept Europe a dimension dividing voters, though not with the same importance as before Brexit got done. In the 84 seats where the party is the principal competitor of the Conservatives, the Liberal Democrats can seek support from Conservative voters who are out of sympathy with the anti-European Tory Party and tactical support from supporters of the also-ran Labour candidate where the Lib Dems are best placed to keep a Tory out.

Although immigration tends to be concentrated in English urban constituencies, it is an issue of nationwide concern, especially in seats where the level of immigration is not high but could grow. The Reform Party has thus been able to mobilise votes nationwide by demanding a reduction in immigration. In 2024 Reform was much more successful in winning votes than in winning seats. Individuals could vote for Reform to express a demand for action to be taken to curb immigration as a Labour government was a foregone conclusion. Thus, Reform finished second in 89 seats.

The Green Party represents a policy dimension relevant in every constituency, but it is not a priority issue for the great majority of voters. The party polls less than 5 per cent of the vote in 279 constituencies and takes as much as 25 per cent of the vote in only eight constituencies. It is a major political threat to Labour in 42 constituencies. In addition, its supporters may tactically vote for an opposition candidate who can cost the Labour government a seat. Conservative seats tend to be immune to the appeal of the Greens; they come second in only two Tory-held constituencies.

In the 71 seats where nationalist parties have become one of the two chief contenders, they introduce another dimension, independence from the United Kingdom. Except in Northern Ireland, voters of a nationalist inclination have a simple choice: they categorically reject all British parties. By contrast, voters who want to maintain the UK as a union of nations must decide which of the British parties on the left or the right best represents their views and which has the best chance of defeating a nationalist candidate.

Four Muslims were elected as independent MPs by emphasising a religious issue – support for Muslims in Gaza – albeit the great majority of British Muslims have come from the Indian sub-continent. They defeated Muslim Labour MPs who gave priority to left–right issues rather than to Palestine. This appeal of particular concern to Muslims is heavily concentrated in a small number of constituencies which have a high proportion of Muslim voters. In 2024 Labour won 16 of the 20 seats with the largest Muslim population (Cracknell and Baker, 2024: 55).

The collective strength of third parties is now great enough to divide constituency competition into seven different dimensions with 26 sub-groups (Table 4.3). None of the non-governing parties was a front-runner in as many as one-sixth of constituencies. This creates major obstacles to breaking the two governing parties' hold on government at the next election. For example, if the Liberal Democrats at the next general election were to win all the seats in which they finished first or second in 2024, the party would have only 93 MPs. A similar showing by the Greens would give them only 44 MPs.

Reform UK is the joker in the pack. If it simply won places where it finished second, usually against Labour, the party would have 103 MPs. Polls show that Reform is now first in popular support nationwide (Appendix Table 3). To become one of the governing parties after the next general election, Nigel Farage would need to combine his personal appeal with support for Reform candidates in hundreds of Labour-held and Conservative-held seats where voters decide they do not want either of the traditional governing parties to take control of the next government.

Citations

Cracknell, Richard and Baker, Carl, 2024. *General Election 2024: Results and Analysis*. London: House of Commons Library Research Briefing.

Prosser, Christopher, 2024. 'Fragmentation revisited: the UK General Election of 2024', *West European Politics*, 48, 6, 1–13.

Rose, Richard and Mackie, Thomas T., 1983. 'Incumbency in government: asset or liability'. In Hans Daalder and Peter Mair, eds, *Western European Party Systems*. London: Sage.

Part II

Where we are now

5

Labour: An early mid-term slump

Winning an election faces a party leader with two challenges. The first starts as soon as the result is confirmed: giving direction to government. The second comes five years later: winning re-election. The two challenges are interdependent, but at a given point in time can pull a prime minister in different directions, for example if a shortfall in government revenue leads to unpopular spending cuts or raising taxes. A new prime minister who enters Downing Street in the middle of a parliament has a head start, as he or she has had up to a decade or more of experience as an MP and minister. While Tony Blair had been an MP for 14 years, he had never been a government minister before becoming prime minister and said he needed years to get a grip on Whitehall.

Keir Starmer came late to Westminster politics. He gained his knighthood for being Director of Public Prosecutions, a non-partisan public office, and did not become an MP until he was 52. After voting for Britain to remain in the EU in the 2016 referendum, he resigned in protest against Jeremy Corbyn's position, only to accept Corbyn's offer of being shadow minister for implementing Brexit. In this role, Starmer successfully led Labour's opposition to Theresa May's terms for withdrawal from the EU.

When Corbyn resigned as party leader after Labour's 2019 election defeat, Keir Starmer stood on a left-wing platform that straddled the gap between the hard left and Tony Blair's New Labour followers. He was elected party leader in a transferable vote ballot with majorities among all three sections of Labour's electoral college. Starmer then spent four years pursuing a single goal: getting into Downing Street (Maguire and Pogrund, 2025). A first step was to distance the party from the left-wing leadership of Jeremy Corbyn. Within months Corbyn was suspended from the party and an election campaign team was assembled under Morgan McSweeney. It concentrated exclusively on electoral politics, as that was the essential precondition for taking control of government.

The 2024 election delivered a mixed blessing: lots of seats but not lots of votes. Thanks to a disproportional electoral system, Labour gained an overwhelming majority in the Commons with a historic low share of the vote. This makes the government safe against by-election defeats and the loss of seats due to individual MPs defecting. However, if Labour loses only a few percentage points in votes at the next general election, it will lose a large number of seats and its electoral majority will be at risk. Opinion polls now show that the government's mid-term slump started two months after it took office rather than after two years of governing.

This chapter charts the decline in Labour's position, beginning with a comparison of changes promised in the Labour manifesto with what voters want. It then documents the many changes that have occurred in the first year and one-half of the Labour government. Some are due to the force of events and many are due to the government's unforced errors. The loss of voter support in the polls and the electoral system threaten to turn Labour's massive majority at the last election into a massive defeat at the next election. The hundreds of Labour MPs worried about losing their seats need not wait until the next election to act. The party's rules give them power to vote Keir Starmer out of office, provided that they can agree on when to challenge his leadership and who should succeed him.

Voters' priorities and Labour's missions

In democratic theory a general election gives voters the power to choose a government to deal with the issues they think are important, and the governing party's victory gives it the legitimacy to implement policies it highlights in its manifesto. Labour manifesto priorities combined some issues that were high in the polls, some that were high within the party and some that were rated highly by both groups.

What voters want

While a government must deal with dozens of issues, ordinary voters usually focus their attention on only a few issues. During the 2024 general election campaign YouGov presented respondents with a list of 16 issues and asked them to identify the three most important issues in deciding how they vote. A big majority of voters named at least two issues as important. A follow-up question then asked voters to identify which issue they saw as most important (Table 5.1).

Voters are selective in the priority they give to issues. They give first priority to issues that can affect their households and themselves. The cost of living, the economy generally and health were each selected as very important by a third or more of respondents and a quarter stressed immigration and asylum-seekers as important. Although housing and taxes affect almost every household, only one-tenth of respondents rate them as electorally important. Household concerns such as family and transportation are not seen as matters important for political choice; they are decided by choice within the household.

When asked to select a single issue as most important, the ranking of issues changed. The cost of living again came first, but immigration moved up to second place, followed by the economy in general and health services. Even though pensions affect upwards of a quarter of voters, they were named as the most important issue by only 3 per cent of voters, as pensioners – like those of working age – gave a much higher priority to the cost of living and health. Education affects nearly half of households but only 1 per cent see this public service as the most important electoral issue.

Table 5.1 Issues influencing voters in 2024 election (%)

Q. Which of the following will be the most important issues in deciding how you will vote at the coming election? Please tick up to three.
Q. Of the following that you said were top issues in deciding how you would vote, which would you say is the SINGLE most important in deciding how you will vote?

	Top three	First importance
Cost of living	45	26
Economy in general	32	16
Health	34	14
Immigration, asylum	26	18
Environment, climate change	14	4
Housing	10	3
Tax	10	3
Crime	9	2
Defence and security	9	2
Relations with the EU	8	2
Pensions	8	3
Education	7	1
Welfare benefits	5	1
Conflict in Gaza	5	2
Family, childcare	4	1
Transport	2	0

Source: YouGov survey of 2,040 respondents, 29–30 May 2024.

There were marked partisan differences in choosing the most important issues. The cost of living was ranked first by 36 per cent of Labour voters compared to 15 per cent of Conservatives and 8 per cent of Reform supporters. As for immigration, 68 per cent of Reform supporters and 27 per cent of Conservatives placed it first, compared to only 3 per cent of Labour voters. Although only 5 per cent thought Gaza was an important issue, it is viewed with a high intensity; among this small group two-fifths think Gaza is the most important issue the British government should deal with.

What Labour promised

The first theme in the 2024 Labour manifesto was expressed in a single world on the cover: Change. Keir Starmer envisioned this rhetorically as going 'further and deeper than New Labour, ... changing our entire culture, our DNA' (quoted in Freedman, 2025: 275). Like the 1964 Labour manifesto declaring 'Let's go with Labour', it did not indicate the direction of change. It modestly echoed John F. Kennedy's vague appeal to turn over a new leaf in politics. To Morgan McSweeney, change meant moving from the office of the leader of the opposition to 10 Downing Street by making Starmer prime minister. To this end there was a picture of Starmer on the cover, one of 33 in the manifesto. Starmer was no match for the photogenic Kennedy.

The Labour manifesto focused on five public policy missions:

- Kick-start economic growth to secure the highest sustained growth of any major G7 country.
- Build an NHS fit for the future where everyone lives well for longer.
- Make Britain a clean energy superpower by delivering cheaper, zero-carbon electricity by 2030 and combating the threat of climate change.

- Take back the streets by halving violent crime and raising confidence in the police and justice system.
- Break down barriers to opportunity for young people.

Of these goals, three – health services, the state of the environment and crime – were important to voters and also could be judged from their own experience. Breaking down barriers for young people was aimed at a select section of the population. Whereas the cost of living can be assessed when people do their weekly shopping, Britain's economic growth in comparison with other countries can be assessed only by reading international comparisons occasionally reported in the quality media.

While government policies can have some influence on all these missions, they are not the only source of outcomes. Public expenditure and taxation are inputs into the national economy along with actions by companies, consumers and international trade and finance. Individuals' health and long life reflect their diet and exercise, socio-economic status and family inheritance as well as medical treatment and public health. The extent of thefts and violent crime depends on what anti-social actors do and on how and whether the police deal with or ignore illegal activities such as shoplifting and drug-dealing. The opportunities of youth are influenced by family background, their community and what they make of the educational opportunities offered by schools. Up to a point, government can control carbon emissions, but funding energy policies depends on economic growth, and global climate change is most influenced by countries with massive economies such as China and the United States.

At the end of the Starmer government's first year in office, *The Times*'s specialist journalists evaluated on a five-point scale Labour's progress towards achieving its goals (Swinford et al., 2025). It gave the highest mark – three out of five – to actions taken in education. Three missions – economic growth, health care and protection of the environment – were given two marks out of five. It gave the lowest mark, one out of five, to its handling of welfare policies directly linked to the lives of millions of voters. Immigration and asylum control, a policy that voters ranked highly but the Labour government initially tried to ignore, was likewise given only one mark out of five.

The most important issues to voters – the economy, health and immigration – have remained the same in this Parliament and so have the government's difficulties in dealing with each issue. Inflation, which immediately impacts voters every time they shop, rose to almost double the target rate, reaching 3.8 per cent by August 2025, and is forecast to remain high (Harari, 2025). Meanwhile, real economic growth has fluctuated between 1.0 and 1.5 per cent, a rate insufficient to provide the tax revenue needed to meet the increase in public expenditure. The multiplicity of health targets results in evidence of positive changes on some measures and negative changes on others (Opie-Martin et al., 2025). Legal immigration has fallen, but much more visible illegal immigration has increased.

Confronted in government with dozens of different policy challenges, the Starmer government has had to expand greatly the number of issues that it must address. Concurrently, it has expanded its vocabulary describing what it does. It has announced more than thirty different priorities including foundations, first steps, milestones and economic pillars. Anxious Labour MPs are asking the prime minister to produce a simple and attractive statement of the Labour government's purpose that can be used in efforts to regain the support of ex-Labour voters.

The force of events and unforced errors

The vagueness of invoking change as a vision had the electoral attraction of a Rorschach inkblot; it allowed voters to read into it what they wanted. However, once Labour was in government this stratagem had the disadvantage of offering little guidance to ministers and senior civil servants about the specific public policies that the Labour government should adopt to achieve its goals. For Keir Starmer, the answer was simple: act pragmatically. A public prosecutor does not plan crimes. Their job is to react to files placed before them and decide pragmatically whether the evidence at hand justifies prosecution.

Immediately on taking office Keir Starmer's government was subject to events that they were forced to respond to. Some events were predictable, such as the need to introduce a budget or deal with illegal immigration. Other events were unpredictable, such as Reform UK overtaking the Conservative Party as Labour's chief electoral competitor. Unforced errors can result from government initiatives such as its proposal to abolish the winter fuel allowance, or from a maladroit response to a revelation about untoward behaviour by a Cabinet minister. Events have force when the government is obligated to act, even if it means taking unpopular but necessary actions or making a pragmatic U-turn.

The force of events

The Labour manifesto described maintaining national security as the first duty of any government but it could hardly anticipate the circumstances in which it was forced to do so by events at home and abroad. They ranged from domestic riots to national security challenges reaching from Moscow and Ukraine to Donald Trump in Washington (Rose, 2025).

A few weeks after Labour entered office, violent anti-immigrant rioting broke out in Southport after an immigrant's offspring was arrested on charges of killing three children. Keir Starmer immediately pledged full support for the police in suppressing violence and arresting those responsible. Within ten days of the riots, 177 people had been convicted and given sentences averaging two years. A fortnight after the rioting ended, a YouGov poll found majorities approved of how the police and courts had handled the riots and a plurality of 43 per cent endorsed how Starmer had acted. In the year since, rioting on the scale of Southport has not recurred.

Illegal immigration across the English Channel accounts for a low proportion of total immigration, but it is a daily and visible sign of the Labour government's inability to meet its manifesto commitment of controlling Britain's borders. In summer 2025, illegal immigration was up by almost half since the previous year. Under pressure from Reform UK, Keir Starmer authorised his staff to prepare a speech in which he warned that, without taking back control of immigration, 'Britain risks becoming an island of strangers rather than a nation'. The statement echoed Enoch Powell's 1968 anti-immigrant 'Rivers of Blood' speech. Starmer expressed ignorance of that similarity and said he had not had time to read the speech carefully before delivering it. The government has since announced stronger measures to deter and deport illegal immigrants; these have yet to show a substantial effect.

A prime minister has an ex-officio responsibility to represent the United Kingdom in international affairs. Engaging with foreign governments is a necessary but not sufficient means of exercising influence. The idea that the British prime minister is at the centre of world affairs is as dead as Winston Churchill. A positive outcome of many meetings is an agreed media statement that calls for third parties to act differently. In dealing with a superpower such as China, dilemmas can arise. For example, when evidence was uncovered of two parliamentary assistants supplying official secrets to the Chinese government, a prosecution was launched and then dropped without adequate explanation.

Keir Starmer has made his presence visible in international affairs. In his first 407 days in office, he spent 67 days in 29 trips abroad plus a significant amount of time preparing for trips. This rate of travel is well above that of his six immediate predecessors. Many trips have been to distant places, such as Western Samoa for a Commonwealth meeting or to Brazil for a G20 meeting. This has left other ministers to make public responses to important issues in his absence and given the prime minister the nickname 'Anywhere but here Keir' (Wright and Maguire, 2025).

The Starmer government has maintained Britain's traditional policy of giving first priority to relations with Washington, a priority not reciprocated by American presidents. In opposition Labour leaders maintained the party's traditional links with the Democratic Party. In 2019 Starmer said, 'An endorsement from Donald Trump tells you everything you need to know about what is wrong with Boris Johnson's politics.' David Lammy, then shadow foreign secretary, described Donald Trump undiplomatically as a 'neo-Nazi-sympathising sociopath'. Labour headquarters organised volunteers to go to the United States to canvass for the Democrats in the 2024 American presidential election.

Once Donald Trump replaced Joe Biden as president, Keir Starmer, with the co-operation of the King, played up to Trump's Scottish roots and his love of royal flattery. However, Trump's love of tariffs is stronger. This is specially relevant to the British economy, since the

United States has been its single biggest national export market. An agreement reached in June 2025 was hailed as a victory, since proposed punitive tariffs were reduced to 10 per cent, a level higher than previously but lower than what Trump announced for EU goods. American enterprises also gained the right to export to Britain beef produced by methods banned here.

The unreliability of American support for Britain's security has been heightened by critical statements about British domestic policy by Trump's entourage. Russia's attack on Ukraine and President Trump's response have raised threats to the security of Europe, including Britain. Trump's readiness to seek a peace deal by direct negotiations between Washington and Moscow has left Britain out of discussions. The prime minister is on the sidelines discussing with the French president and the German chancellor what to do if a peace deal imperils not only Ukraine but also the security of all of Europe. The immediate answer is: not much. The longer-term answer is for Britain to create a properly equipped military force that can be part of a European defence community of willing nations from France to Poland.

Fearful of giving an opening to Tory and Reform anti-Europeans, the Labour manifesto (2024: 117f) said of Britain's relations with the European Union: 'We must make Brexit work.' However, the red lines it set on trade negotiations included, 'There will be no return to the single market, the customs union, or freedom of movement.' These conditions rule out a significant agreement since they are inconsistent with what the

EU requires for granting the concessions that the government seeks. When senior ministers suggest that rejoining the EU's customs union could give a much-needed boost to British growth, Keir Starmer has been quick to rule it out. A meeting with EU officials about improving British trade damaged by Brexit is described as successful if it leads to another meeting that avoids a breakdown in discussions that would be a sign of failure.

Unforced errors

Government ministers do not intend to make errors, but they do nonetheless. Unlike failures in response to forced events, unforced errors may arise from actions that ministers voluntarily take, such as Tony Blair's decision to join the United States in going to war in Iraq. Unforced errors can also arise from mistakes in planning and implementation, such as massive delays and cost overruns of biilions of pounds in major infrastructure projects such as the HS2 rail line between London and Birmingham.

Once Labour was due to become the government, this attracted wealthy donors whose generous gifts brought with them accusations of sleaze. Lord Alli, a wealthy fundraiser for the Labour Party, gave Keir Starmer and leading shadow ministers expensive clothes and tickets to pop concerts. Starmer insisted it was customary for leading MPs to receive such benefits and that no rules were broken. As the media revelations of gifts dripped out, a U-turn was done. Starmer, the deputy leader and the chancellor of the Exchequer announced they would no longer accept clothes from donors. In a YouGov poll, 59 per cent described the Labour government as sleazy, and the median respondent said it was just as sleazy as the Conservative government it replaced.

A year later the media revealed that Deputy Leader Angela Rayner, who was also the housing minister, had acted without expert legal advice to save herself £40,000 in second-home taxes when buying an £800,000 flat in East Sussex. Initially Keir Starmer backed her. However, when the Independent Adviser on Ministerial Standards found that Rayner had not acted in keeping with the highest standards, she resigned and said she would pay the extra tax. The newly appointed British ambassador to Washington, Lord Peter Mandelson, came under attack when files revealed that he had given gushing support to a convicted billionaire paedophile. Starmer initially backed Mandelson, only to dismiss him the next day when further embarrassing details were made public that had already been in Downing Street's possession.

As progress in electioneering brought Labour within months of gaining control of government, Keir Starmer gave the first sign of preparing for governing. He appointed a former senior civil servant, Sue Gray, as his chief of staff to produce plans for giving direction to senior Whitehall officials once Labour entered government (Maguire and Pogrund, 2025: 295ff, 415ff). Gray followed Starmer into Downing Street at a salary higher than the prime minister. However, there was no avalanche of measures for Starmer to release in the first hundred days to show he was in charge, as President Trump had done. Inexperienced Labour ministers were left to fend for themselves without direction from the prime minister's office. In the words of a Starmer associate, 'Labour's preparations for government existed primarily in Sue Gray's mind.' Ten weeks after the government was formed, Gray was pushed out of Downing Street and given a place in the House of Lords.

The lack of direction from Downing Street has continued since. Starmer's appointment of Sir Chris Wormald as Cabinet secretary to push the government's programme through Whitehall departments was the object of critical briefings by political appointees in Number 10 and what he has and has not done since has kept up critical briefings against him, creating what a demoralised senior civil servant described as 'a nest of vipers' (Parker and Pickard, 2025). By September 2025 Keir Starmer had had four heads of communications and was bringing in expert economic special advisers, hoping that more staff would create more progress. By autumn, policy advisers and some ministers were briefing journalists that the problem was not staffing and organisation but political. Starmer has not laid out a vision or ideology that gives guidance to Cabinet ministers about the government's goals.

In the belief that the difficulty in implementing Labour government policy was Whitehall's unresponsive institutions, in September 2025 Keir Starmer created the post of Chief Secretary to the Prime Minister 'to support the delivery of the Prime Minister's priorities and the Government's Plan for Change' and appointed an MP, Darren Jones, to the post. Three months later Jones told the Commons public administration committee that the government had become 'addicted to making announcements' and needed to refocus on delivering outcomes. He described as a high-priority outcome the creation of more interesting social media platforms for communicating with ordinary citizens.

A series of pragmatic decisions taken without reference to fixed principles has resulted in 14 U-turns, as decisions that appeared suitable when made created a furore in Labour ranks, and Downing Street sought to still it by reversing its decision. For example, criminal convictions in Labour strongholds of ethnic Asian men on charges of grooming young girls for sexual exploitation led to demands for setting up a national inquiry. Keir Starmer rejected doing so, saying that the demand came from groups 'jumping on the far right bandwagon'. A report on the gangs by Baroness Casey of Blackstock then confirmed that Asian men and asylum-seekers were substantially over-represented in grooming gangs and that the police had responded inadequately 'for fear of appearing racist'. Starmer then did a U-turn, promptly authorising a full national inquiry. In October 2025 the inquiry fell into disarray after victims of grooming gangs withdrew their participation fearing it would be a cover-up, and potential chairs of the inquiry withdrew their names from consideration.

Trying to deal with the economy

The Starmer government's management of the economy has combined unforced errors and U-turns. It made an unqualified manifesto pledge: 'Labour will not increase taxes on working people.' It also put spending on public policies in a fiscal straitjacket: 'Our fiscal rules are non-negotiable and will apply to every decision taken by a Labour government. This means that the current budget must move into balance, so that day-to-day costs are met by revenues and debt must be falling.'

Less than a month after taking office, Chancellor of the Exchequer Rachel Reeves announced that the government would cut a winter fuel allowance introduced by Gordon Brown that paid ten million pensioners between £100 and £300 each year. The reason given was the need to deal with a large deficit left by the Conservatives. To backbench Labour MPs it was the abandonment of a significant Labour social benefit. As one MP put it, 'We weren't elected to take away benefits from people.' Starmer dismissed MPs' demands to abandon the cuts as 'noises off'. In June 2025 there was a U-turn: the winter fuel allowance was restored for 7.5 million pensioners. Doing so has boosted the appetite of Labour MPs for more government U-turns on measures going against traditional Labour values.

A total of £4.8 billion in cuts in the payment of disability grants to millions of recipients was announced in June 2025 to meet a fiscal priority. This triggered fresh opposition from Labour MPs, all of whom had disabled constituents threatened with the loss of a significant benefit. More than 120 Labour MPs signed motions opposing the cuts. The whips appealed to MPs' self-interest by telling them their opposition jeopardised any chance of a ministerial appointment and could cost them their right to stand as a Labour candidate at the next election. In the lead-up to a key Commons debate in June 2025, the government began making concessions. Just 90 minutes before the Speaker was due to call a vote, the government made a full U-turn, withdrawing key parts of the cuts.

The first Rachel Reeves budget in October 2024 increased taxes by £40 billion, principally on business, to fill a budget black hole blamed on artful accounting by Conservative predecessors. It also raised public spending by almost £70 billion. In an attempt to reassure business, she told a Confederation of British Industry conference, 'I'm not coming back with more borrowing or more taxes' (quoted in Parker, Borrett and Giles, 2025).

In the months leading up to the November 2025 budget there were strong pressures to increase spending on commitments to pensioners and debt interest as well a need to increase spending on the wage bill of Britain's biggest employer, the National Health Service. Moreover, the independent Office for Budget Responsibility was forecasting that, even after allowing for the boost that inflation was giving to tax revenue, it was not rising fast enough to meet the total cost of public spending. Reeves and Keir Starmer began flying kites indicating the prospect of increasing income tax to meet the prospective deficit. In the event, adjustment to Office of Budget Responsibility forecasts led to the abandonment of a proposed increase in income tax.

The 2026–27 budget was launched with something for everybody. Keir Starmer boasted that the U-turn lifting the two-child limit on cap on benefits would significantly reduce child poverty. A smorgasbord of tax changes immediately added £26 billion to public revenue; public borrowing is rising too. Income tax will rise by stealth up to 2031, as the threshold levels at which it is levied are frozen rather than adjusted for inflation. This will increase the taxes that people at all levels of income will actually pay. YouGov's post-budget poll found 50 per cent thought the budget would leave them worse off compared to 3 per cent expecting it to make them better off. Weeks after the budget the government made another U-turn. It greatly narrowed the impact of a proposed inheritance tax on farms after more than forty Labour MPs abstained in a vote on imposing the tax on big majority of family farms.

Delaying expenditure avoids the political backlash of taking away benefits since no money has been spent. Since military defence is not one of Labour's five leading missions, it is an easy target for delay. The party's manifesto (2024: 15) claimed, 'As the party that founded NATO [*sic*], ... we [will] meet our [NATO] obligations in full.' The party has stated the ambition that defence spending will reach 3 per cent of GDP in the next Parliament (that is, before 2035), subject to economic and fiscal conditions. Meanwhile, under pressure from President Trump, European members of NATO have accepted a target of spending 5 per cent of GDP on defence.

The Starmer government's U-turns and a 'spend now, pay later' budget have the pragmatic justification of temporarily pacifying Labour MPs unhappy with Rachel Reeves and Keir Starmer donning fiscal straitjackets. However, they go against the political logic of adopting unpopular decisions at the beginning of a five-year term in office in order to have more room for increased spending when the next election approaches. Instead, by 2029 voters will find themselves squeezed by stealth taxes that will double the marginal rate of tax for millions of workers and the cumulative effect of five years of inflation on their cost of living.

What voters see

Labour's efforts to deliver its missions and respond to events and unforced errors are creating a detailed record of what the Labour government has and has not achieved. However, voters do not follow what government does in detail, and Keir Starmer's inability to articulate a clear vision of what his government is doing makes it hard for voters to see the overall purpose of the Starmer government, a view shared by many Labour MPs.

At the end of Labour's first year in office, the Lord Ashcroft Polls (2025) asked respondents: *Do you understand what the Labour government under Keir Starmer is trying to do?* In response 50 per cent said they did not understand what the government was trying to do, and an additional 12 per cent simply replied don't know. Among the minority who had an idea of what the government was doing, more than three-quarters did not like what they saw, while only 9 per cent both understood and approved of the Labour government's efforts.

Whether people are interested in politics or not, a big majority are exposed at least intermittently to news

Table 5.2 What voters recall Labour has done (%)

Q. Since it was elected last July, can you name anything specific the Starmer government has done, whether you agreed with it or not?	
Means-tested winter fuel allowance	38
Cut disability benefits	11
Increased employer's National Insurance contributions	8
Allowed more illegal immigrants in	6
Made several U-turns	6
Charged VAT on private school fees	4
Changed inheritance tax	3
Signed three trade deals	4
Increased defence spending	3
Reduced NHS waiting lists	3

Source: Lord Ashcroft Polls, 2025. Eight per cent could not remember anything the government had done.

about what government does. When asked to name anything specific done by the Starmer government in its first year in office, 92 per cent remembered something (Table 5.2). The great majority of recollections were negative. The most frequently cited actions were cuts to cash benefits paid to pensioners and those with disabilities. Three different types of tax increases were recalled by 15 per cent. An additional 6 per cent associated the Starmer government with an increase in illegal immigrants, and the same proportion saw it making multiple U-turns. Only 10 per cent saw the Starmer government doing positive things in its first year.

A reduction in NHS waiting lists, a major government mission, was recalled by 3 per cent of respondents. By

December 2025 the Ashcroft Poll found that 5 per cent were seeing NHS waiting lists falling. It also found that policies of special interest to Labour's traditional voters were beginning to be noticed: 5 per cent recalled that the Labour government had increased the minimum wage and 4 per cent that it had improved workers' rights.

Voters wield a double-edged sword

A party in government has the advantage of being in a position to campaign for re-election by delivering what the voters who put them there want. However, the double-edged sword that voters hold can also cut the other way. When a governing party fails to meet its voters' expectations, it cannot escape blame for actions it has taken. In its second year in office, the force of events and unforced errors have inflicted multiple electoral cuts on the Starmer government.

Unpopular with the electorate

As the winner of the 2024 general election, Labour had a head start in the polls. However, its share of the national vote was the lowest on record for any winner of a parliamentary majority. Labour did not win the election because the electorate favoured its policies and leader. Its vote went up barely 1 percentage point from that gained under Jeremy Corbyn's leadership in 2019. Keir Starmer won because voters turned against the Conservative government. The weakness of its support was quickly demonstrated as the Starmer government's actions stimulated the development of anti-government voters.

Labour's support in the polls started low and sank fast. Within a month its average support fell below its general election level, and by October 2024 it had fallen below 30 per cent (see Appendix Table 3). Labour dropped into second place behind Reform UK in April 2025. Continued decline brought support for Labour below 23 per cent one year after its election victory, an unprecedented fall for a recent election winner. In the autumn, Labour's support averaged 19 per cent in monthly polls, a level at which it risked dropping into third place behind the Conservatives.

Public approval of Keir Starmer has fallen in parallel with approval of the Labour government. Immediately after entering Downing Street, 44 per cent approved of Starmer in a YouGov poll, albeit a greater number, 47 per cent, expressed disapproval. Since then, positive approval of Starmer has fallen and disapproval has consistently been higher than approval. By May 2025 Starmer's personal approval rating had fallen as low as 23 per cent, and by December 2025 only 13 per cent were satisfied with the way Starmer was doing his job. This was the lowest rating recorded by Ipsos for any prime minister since it started asking the question in 1977 (see Table 2.1).

The Starmer government's first electoral test, local elections in England in May 2025, confirmed its weak hold on the electorate. Since Labour had done badly in the previous round of local contests, it had a limited number of council seats at stake. Nonetheless, the result was bad for Labour; it lost 189 seats. Reform UK did best: it won County Durham, which Labour had controlled since 1925, along with many council seats taken from Labour. On the same day Labour also lost a by-election to Reform, where it was defending its sixth safest seat. In October a Welsh Senedd by-election in Caerphilly, a constituency that had been Labour for more than a century, left the Labour candidate trailing behind Plaid Cymru and Reform UK with 11 per cent of the vote.

When the Ipsos Monitor on the eve of the 2025 Labour Party conference asked, *How satisfied or dissatisfied are you with the way the government is running the country?*, 82 per cent said they were dissatisfied. The 13 per cent satisfied with Labour's performance were less than two-fifths the proportion who had voted Labour at the general election.

Losing support to left and right

At the 2024 general election Labour benefited from the division of the vote among multiple non-governing parties. Since then, half of Labour's support has fragmented to parties on both the left and the right (Table 5.3). Together, the Green Party and Liberal Democrats have attracted two-thirds of Labour defectors. In political science language, such shifts do not mean Labour voters are abandoning their left-of-centre views. They are simply changing which party on the left they support. The Green Party is benefiting more by offering a left-wing alternative to the Starmer

Table 5.3 Current voting intention of 2024 Labour voters in 2025 (%)

Labour		51
	Left (31)	
Green		16
Liberal Democrat		15
	Right (14)	
Reform UK		10
Conservative		4
Nationalists, others		4

Source: YouGov survey of 2,033 respondents, 7–8 December 2025.

government, while the Liberal Democrats benefit from disaffected Labour moderates who do not want to vote for a right-wing party. An additional 4 per cent express support for nationalists and new groups on the left. Two parties on the right, Reform UK and the Conservatives, have gained the support of more than one-quarter of Labour defectors, with Nigel Farage's party the principal beneficiary.

While Labour is losing more votes to parties on the left, it also faces the prospect of losing seats to parties on the right. Both Reform UK and the Conservatives can win seats without gaining significant support from Labour because more than four-fifths of the seats Labour is defending were won with less than half the vote in 2024. Thus, the defection of Labour voters to the left in large numbers makes it easier for a Reform or Conservative candidate to combine right-wing voters and non-voters to take seats that Labour holds with only a plurality of a constituency's vote.

After Reform UK came first in the 2025 local elections, Downing Street decided to treat Reform as its principal electoral threat. Keir Starmer has called Nigel Farage's promise of generous spending on welfare benefits 'fantasy economics'. In an atypical burst of rhetoric, Starmer told the 2025 Labour Party conference that the party's opposition was 'a fight for the soul of the country'. The Starmer government's proposals to reduce legal and illegal immigration have taken the fight against Reform to the latter's home ground. While there is no limit on what Farage can promise, Labour's claim to be an effective anti-immigration party depends on what the government actually delivers.

Labour MPs hold the sword of Damocles

Since the 411 MPs in the Parliamentary Labour Party are more than three times the size of the official Opposition and 80 times that of Reform UK, the chief parliamentary opposition that Keir Starmer needs to worry about is from MPs within the Labour Party. When asked by a committee of MPs about his biggest disappointment after 18 months in office, he said, 'The ability to get things done in Parliament' (Parker, Pickard and Sheppard, 2025). An analysis of what happened to Labour's 35 legislative proposals in its initial King's Speech found that 18 months later a majority had yet to become Acts of Parliament (Kelly, 2025).

Unlike the French president Emmanuel Macron, Keir Starmer is not directly elected by a popular vote. Instead, he is elected by a two-tier electoral college of

Labour Party members in which MPs have the initiative. They also have the power to bring down on Starmer's head the sword of Damocles – a vote to replace him as leader and prime minister – whenever they can agree it is time to do so.

Up to a point, a prime minister can use the power of patronage to maintain support. Moreover, one-quarter of Labour MPs can be given official posts in the government on condition that they loyally support whatever the Starmer government is doing, including its unforced errors. Up to half again this number show loyalty to the prime minister in the hope of getting a government appointment in the next reshuffle.

An absolute majority of Labour MPs elected in 2024 were new to Parliament and unfamiliar with government ministries. They did not join the Labour Party to support Keir Starmer or any particular leader but to support traditional Labour social welfare policies. During their time as party members they have seen many Labour leaders come and go. They spent 14 years campaigning at the local level to reverse the effect of Conservative austerity policies. Since then, the polls have undermined a major weapon that the whips normally use to enforce discipline: losing re-nomination as a Labour candidate if they do not back the government. Labour's deep slump in the polls threatens a majority of Labour MPs with losing their seat at the next election because they do support an unpopular Labour government.

While any government with a substantial majority can ignore a small number of individual rebels, it is risky to do so when a rebellion threatens a large number of Labour MPs either publicly abstaining or voting against their party whip. Opposition from masses of backbench MPs has led to the government making U-turns on its proposals to take away fuel allowances to pensioners and benefits of disability claimants.

The strength of dissatisfaction with the Starmer government was shown in the vote for a new deputy leader in October 2025. Lucy Powell, dismissed as a Cabinet minister, stood as the candidate of backbench MPs against Bridget Phillipson, a Cabinet minister bound to support government policy whatever it was. Powell campaigned for members' votes by stressing that as a backbench MP she would speak for the party not the government, and press it to maintain traditional Labour values. Phillipson stressed that she would be a voice for party members within government. Powell was elected deputy leader with 54 per cent of the votes cast by party members.

Labour MPs disaffected by the policies of the Starmer government, the polls and election results have a choice between changing their party or changing their party's leader. Plans for a new Your Party advocating socialist values were announced in July 2025, with former Labour leader Jeremy Corbyn and independent MPs as members. It initially attracted supporters and cash donations to its website, but has faced a public dispute between Corbyn and Zarah Sultana, a Midlands MP who describes herself as its co-leader. The disputes continued at a November conference to launch the party. It adopted a novel collective leadership rule stating that no MP was eligible for a leadership post (see chapter 8).

The simplest way to change the Labour government's direction is to change its leader and thus the country's prime minister. By the time of the Labour Party's autumn 2025 conference, backbench MPs and some Cabinet ministers were ready to give journalists off-the-record briefings on the need for a new leader. In an attempt to stop these briefings, sources close to Keir Starmer went public, saying he would fight any attempt to depose him.

Since Downing Street aides admitted that talk about replacing Keir Starmer as prime minister is rife, the discussion about who could replace him is now out in the open. The names of two Cabinet ministers feature prominently. Wes Streeting, the health minister, has openly declared his ambition to be prime minister some day. He is a much better communicator than Starmer and much more experienced in Labour politics. Ed Miliband, the energy minister and former Labour leader, has demonstrated the ability to win the support of Labour Party members, whose votes decide the party leadership. As a backbench MP, Angela Rayner can distance herself from government measures unpopular with her left-wing following. Andy Burnham has put himself forward as a soft-left candidate who won re-election as mayor of Greater Manchester with 63 per cent of the vote. However, to stand for party leader Burnham must win a by-election giving him a seat in the House of Commons.

A Labour Party briefing describes the system for challenging an incumbent party leader as a bit complicated. This is in keeping with the federal structure of the Labour Party and with the interest of a Labour prime minister. At least 20 per cent of MPs must nominate a candidate to challenge the prime minister. Unlike a parliamentary vote of no confidence, party rules require one or more politicians to challenge the incumbent leader in order for a ballot to be held. This could be done by a member of Starmer's Cabinet first resigning on an issue favoured by traditional Labour MPs or by Angela Rayner deciding the time is right to trigger a leadership election. Leadership candidates require their nomination to be endorsed by up to 82 MPs and 5 per cent of constituency parties or three affiliated bodies such as trade unions. The 2025 election of a left-wing critic of the Starmer government as general secretary of Unison, Britain's largest union, will ensure significant trade union support for a left-wing candidate pledged to pursue a strongly left-wing policy favouring trade unionists.

The right to vote on the leader and de facto prime minister is in the hands of individual party members and affiliated supporters. This is much larger than the number eligible to vote for the Conservative Party leader, but barely 4 per cent of Labour's vote at the last general election. The winner requires an absolute majority of the vote. If there are three or more candidates, voting is by a preferential ballot, in which candidates are ranked in order of preference. If no candidate secures an absolute majority in the vote, second and lower preferences are transferred until one candidate gets a majority.

At the start of 2026 there is an inclination to give Keir Starmer a bit more time to show where his policies are leading. A host of elections in May will add ballot-box evidence to what the polls are showing. Labour is on the defensive in London and in English local government elections. There are elections for the devolved Welsh Senedd where Reform UK and Plaid Cymru are challenging Labour's position. In Scotland the Labour Party's association with an unpopular government in London is frustrating hope of winning Scottish government from the Scottish National Party.

Given low expectations, Keir Starmer's best hope for avoiding an immediate leadership challenge would be for local elections in 2026 not to be so bad as expected. In a step to make this happen, the Labour government announced plans to delay up to 63 local council and mayoral elections in England for a year or two in order to give priority to local government re-organisation. The Electoral Commission called the move 'disappointing', the Liberal Democrat leader described it as a 'stitch up' and Nigel Farage said it was the action of a 'banana republic'.

Labour did a U-turn allowing elections to go ahead. Starmer is also hoping that would-be successors cannot agree on the timing of a leadership ballot. For challengers, calculations of timing are not only about gaining enough votes to oust Starmer but also about winning enough votes to put themselves in Downing Street.

Citations

Freedman, Sam, 2025. *Failed State: Why Britain Doesn't Work and How We Fix It*. London: Pan Books.

Harari, Daniel, 2025. *Economic Update: Why Has Inflation Gone Up in 2025?* London: House of Commons Library Insight.

Kelly, Richard, 2025. '2024 King's Speech: progress of legislation'. London: House of Commons Library Research Briefing, 4 December.

Labour Manifesto, 2024. *Change*. London: Labour Party.
Lord Ashcroft Polls, 2025. 'Leaders' grades for the year', 8 July, lordashcroftpolls.com/2025/07/leaders-grades-for-the-year-iran-defence-spending-farage-and-non-doms-and-who-regrets-their-2024-vote. Accessed 21 December 2025.
Maguire, Patrick and Pogrund, Gabriel, 2025. *Get In: The Inside Story of Labour Under Starmer*. London: Bodley Head.
Opie-Martin, Sarah et al., 2025. *One Year On: Is the Government on Track to Meet Its Waiting Times Pledge?* London: Health Foundation.
Parker, George, Borrett, Amy and Giles, Chris, 2025. 'Reeves' "ironclad" rules become a fiscal straitjacket', *Financial Times*, 28 May.
Parker, George and Pickard, Jim, 2025. 'Downing Street "nest of vipers" unleashed on top civil servant', *Financial Times*, 26 October.
Parker, George, Pickard, Jim and Sheppard, David, 2025. 'PM admits whispers over leadership coup "rife"', *Financial Times*, 16 December.
Rose, Richard, 2025. *European Security from Ukraine to Washington*. London: Bloomsbury.
Swinford, Stephen et al., 2025. 'A year into power is Starmer keeping promises?', *The Times*, 5 July.
Wright, Oliver and Maguire, Patrick, 2025. '"Anywhere but here Keir" clocks up 100k air miles', *The Times*, 16 August 2025.
YouGov, 2024. 'What are the most important issues for voters', https://yougov.co.uk/politics/articles/49594-general-election-2024-what-are-the-most-important-issues-for-voters. Accessed 21 December 2025.

6

The Conservative dilemma

When the Conservatives entered government in 2010, prime Minister David Cameron promised to fix a Britain broken after 13 years of Labour rule. Its first priority, reducing the claim of public expenditure on GDP, was initially achieved. The chancellor of the Exchequer, George Osborne, led an austerity programme that reduced public spending on policies affecting many millions of people. Cameron resigned after losing the Brexit referendum in 2016. His successor as prime minister, Theresa May, failed to deliver Brexit. Boris Johnson then delivered Brexit and much else that brought him into disrepute. Liz Truss destroyed the Tory reputation for managing the economy with a budget that wilted as fast as a lettuce. Her successor, Rishi Sunak, was unable to get the government out of the hole it was in. After 14 years of Conservative government, 84 per cent of YouGov respondents described public services as in a bad state. Labour won a much bigger majority than Cameron had by campaigning against the Conservative government's failure to fix a broken Britain (Rayson, 2024: part II).

The loss of more than seven million votes at the 2024 general election left the Conservative Party with the fewest MPs in its history, 121. There were 70 losses to non-governing parties, including 60 to the Liberal Democrats. Twelve Cabinet ministers plus former prime minister Liz Truss lost their seats. In a six-party competition for votes, the party lost support on all sides. One-quarter of its 2019 vote went to Reform UK, whose leaders it had once dismissed as far-right loonies. It also lost votes to the Liberal Democrats and to Labour. The Conservatives are the smallest official Opposition in the House of Commons since 1931.

The Conservatives are now competing with Reform UK on the right and the Liberal Democrats to the centre-left. This faces the party with a dilemma. Should it try to regain defectors from Reform by moving to the right, thereby writing off hopes of regaining defectors from the Liberal Democrats and Labour? Or should it move towards the centre in an effort to regain defectors from the Liberal Democrats and the Labour Party, thereby writing off hopes of regaining defectors from Reform? A simple count of voter support suggests that there is more to gain from moving to the right as Reform is now leading in opinion polls. However, a count of seats points in the opposite direction. If the Conservatives are to win a parliamentary majority, the party must take more than two hundred seats from Labour and the Liberal Democrats; Reform can offer only five seats. However, it has more ex-Conservative voters.

While the Conservatives have been one of Britain's two governing parties for more than a century and one-half, the next section shows that this is today an ambiguous legacy. Failings of the last Conservative government resulted in almost half of its supporters defecting in 2024. The second section sets out the challenges facing the Conservatives in seeking to win votes on opposing fronts. The concluding section shows that a leadership faced with an unwelcome strategic dilemma is pursuing the strategy of Mr Micawber in Dickens's *David Copperfield*: it is waiting for something to turn up.

Massive Conservative defections

When the Conservative Party went into the 2024 general election it was defending a 14-year record of government. The first decade went well: the party's share of the vote rose as it won four successive elections, reaching a peak in Boris Johnson's 2019 victory. However, after it got Brexit done, the Conservative government's response to events and its unforced errors offered supporters many reasons to defect.

A centrifugal defeat

At the 2024 election the Conservative Party lost 47 per cent of the voters who had backed it four years earlier. Defectors flew off in many directions. The activities of the Conservative government offered supporters a multitude of reasons for taking their votes elsewhere. Shortly before election day in 2024 a survey of Conservative defectors asked them to select up to three choices

Table 6.1 Reasons 2019 Tory voters defected in 2024 election (%)

Q. Which of the following are the main reasons for your choice not to vote Conservative? Up to three choices permitted.

	Defected to	
	Lab–Lib	Reform
Bad management		
General failure to deliver	62	44
Incompetence	47	34
Conservatives too divided	17	12
Policies		
No control of immigration	26	72
National Health Service problems	44	30
Bad economic management	29	9
Ideology, personality		
Prefer Johnson to Sunak	15	29
Not Conservative enough	2	23
Too right-wing	8	0

Source: Electoral Calculus and Find Out Now, Conservative Defector survey, 921 respondents, 3–4 June 2025. Lab–Lib includes a small number of defectors to Green Party.

from a list of nine explanations for no longer voting Conservative. The defectors' replies fell into three categories: bad management, policy failures, and ideology and leaders' personalities. A majority gave at least two reasons for not voting Tory (Table 6.1).

Defectors to Reform UK were specially motivated by the failure of five successive Conservative prime ministers to control immigration. It was named by 72 per cent of this group, eight times more often than the Conservative government's economic failings. A generalised failure to deliver policies and incompetence also encouraged defections to Reform, which could not be blamed for failing in government because it had never been in office. Almost one-quarter of Tory defectors also complained that the Conservatives were not conservative enough. Even more were put off voting for the party that had Rishi Sunak as its leader rather than Boris Johnson.

Defectors to the Liberal Democrats and Labour were most encouraged to change parties by the failure of Conservative governments to deliver policies, cited by 62 per cent, and by general incompetence, a complaint of 47 per cent. Problems in the National Health Service and bad economic management were identified as policy faults too. By contrast with defectors to Reform, barely a quarter of defectors to the centre-left emphasised the failure of the Conservative government to control immigration. For this group, divisions within the Conservative Party were more often cited as off-putting than matters of ideology or the personalities of leaders.

Another change of leaders

Given his responsibility for the Conservative election defeat, Rishi Sunak promptly resigned, opening the gates for a leadership election. A number of potential candidates from the outgoing government could not stand because they had lost their seats. Six MPs were nominated for the daunting post of rebuilding a party divided about which direction to head. Three were identified with the party's right wing, Kemi Badenoch, Robert

Jenrick and Priti Patel; two had a centrist inclination, James Cleverly and Tom Tugendhat; and Mel Stride sought to straddle the divide.

MPs voted in early September 2024 to reduce the number of candidates to four. Stride and Patel were eliminated. The four remaining candidates had a month to address their appeals to party audiences and the annual Conservative Party conference. After a month of campaigning, MPs voted again to reduce the alternatives to a pair of candidates. The two moderate candidates, Cleverly and Tugendhat, were both eliminated, and Conservative Party members were then given the power to choose between Badenoch and Jenrick. Kemi Badenoch won the race for party leadership with 55 per cent of the members' vote. She became the party's fourth woman leader and its second leader from an ethnic minority. Notwithstanding its commitment to diversity in representation, the Labour Party has had neither a female nor an ethnic-minority leader.

Seeking votes from opposing sides

While a Conservative Party leader is chosen by party members, a Conservative prime minister needs the support of the electorate. After suffering its lowest vote in its history in 2024, Conservative support has fallen further (Difford, 2025a). Because it gets much more support from older rather than younger voters, the party needs to replace some voters lost through the demographic turnover in the electorate. Furthermore, its support in the polls has declined a fifth during this

Parliament (see Appendix Table 3). As non-governing parties collectively won the biggest share of the national vote, the Conservatives do not need to convert Labour supporters to achieve a substantial increase in votes.

The Conservatives can try to appeal for votes by campaigning on issues that the public believes they will be good at handling. However, the disruption of the party system has made this difficult because six parties now claim they are the best. When YouGov asked voters to identify which party was best able to handle ten different issues, between one-third and almost one-half did not know any party they were confident in (Difford, 2025b). The Conservatives were chosen as best able to handle two issues – the economy and taxation – by 19 per cent of respondents. This was less than half the 41 per cent who thought no party would do well on taxation and the 43 per cent with no confidence in any party's economic management.

A major problem for the Conservatives is that Nigel Farage has been quick to take advantage of Reform UK's ideological closeness to seize the right-wing political agenda, endorsing a massive reduction in immigration, a goal the previous Conservative government failed to achieve. Furthermore, the inertia of current Reform supporters creates substantial resistance to moving to the Conservatives. An October 2025 YouGov survey found that 90 per cent of Reform voters in the general election were still supporting the party, compared to 61 per cent of Conservatives still favouring the Tories. Reform UK supporters are not apolitical floating voters but people who have consciously rejected the Tories.

The argument that Reform UK cannot govern because it has no experience of government is counterbalanced by it not being associated with the failings of the last Conservative government.

The alternative of appealing to centre and left voters is consistent with Harold Macmillan's claim that the Conservatives are a cross-class One Nation party. In 2019 Boris Johnson's appeal to 'Get Brexit done' forged a one-off gain of seats in North of England Labour constituencies that voted Brexit and in South of England constituencies that rejected Jeremy Corbyn's left-wing views. However, Johnson also ended the division between pro-Brexit and pro-EU Tory MPs by expelling a score of the latter, who tended to be One Nation Tories. This removed the appeal of the Conservative Party to centre-left voters as well as the pressure within the party to move towards the centre. However, there remain electoral incentives for the Conservatives to seek votes from the three left-of-centre parties.

As the alternative governing party, the Conservatives should be well placed to benefit from a collapse in popular support for the governing party, as Labour did prior to the 2024 election. However, the political distance between the Conservatives and disillusioned left-of-centre voters is an obstacle. On the left–right scale, the average Labour voter is 65 points distant from the average Conservative voter. By contrast, the average Tory is only 6 points distant from the average Reform supporter (Figure 3.1).

The Conservative dilemma is that, while the party is better positioned to gain votes from Reform UK, the seats it needs to win are principally held by Labour. At the 2024 general election the Conservatives were trailing Reform UK in only nine seats, while second to Labour in 219 seats. Labour won the great majority of its seats with a plurality rather than a majority of the vote. For the Conservatives to take lots of seats from Labour it needs to convince right-wing voters that it is the party best placed to turn out a Labour government. While this claim is justified by the results of the 2024 election, current opinion polls show that Reform UK is better placed than the Conservatives to unseat Labour MPs. This is an incentive for Conservative supporters to defect to Reform to turn the Labour government out of office.

Whose side is time on?

A party that has just lost an election needs time to recover, especially when its defeat is as big as that the Tories experienced in 2024. It took the Conservatives two more election defeats to regain control of government in 2010 after suffering a lesser defeat to Labour in 1997. After losing office in 1979 it took Labour three more defeats before it returned to Downing Street.

A theme of Kemi Badenoch's leadership is that the party needs time to reflect on the reasons for the party's defeat and to craft an appeal that not only gets immediate headline attention but also has a lasting effect. This strategy is consistent with the fact that the next general election is not due until 2029. However, it is inconsistent with the fact that competition for support is now being conducted on a 24-hour-a-day, seven-day-a-week basis in all kinds of media, and Nigel Farage has exploited the opportunities this offers to Reform's advantage.

Defections of voters continue

The maxim 'Opposition parties don't win elections, government loses them' implies that a losing party must wait until the government's slump gives it the opportunity to regain the support it has lost. The unprecedented early collapse in support for the Labour government has offered the Conservatives an immediate chance to overtake Labour and come first in the polls. This did not happen (see Appendix Table 3). Labour's loss of support in its first six months in office was not matched by a significant Conservative gain. In December 2024 Labour had dropped 7 percentage points in the polls but was still 3 points ahead of the Conservatives because the latter's support had not changed since the general election. Reform UK has been the chief beneficiary of Labour's fall.

Conservative support began to decline in the monthly average of polls in February 2025, when it reached 22 per cent. It was pushed into third place as Reform began to come first in opinion polls ahead of Labour. Local elections in May 2025 confirmed the Conservatives' weakness. The party lost more than six hundred councillors and control of 16 councils, principally to Reform UK. By September the party's average poll support was down to 17 per cent, and single polls sometimes gave it only 15 per cent. By December 2025 it had recovered a little but was still one-fifth lower than its 2024 election result.

While the Conservative Party has retained its position as the official Opposition because it is the second-largest party in Parliament, it is struggling to avoid being relegated to third place in terms of electoral support behind Reform UK and Labour. The party's fall in the polls has reached a point at which the first-past-the-post electoral system works against it, giving it a smaller share of MPs than of votes. Statistical analyses of the constituency impact of its loss of national support indicate that a lower vote could reduce it to 50 or fewer MPs if an election were held at present. This would leave it in fourth place in the Commons behind the Liberal Democrats. In a worst-case analysis, it is threatened with falling into fifth place in MPs if the Scottish National Party surges (see Table 9.1).

Conservative support has fallen because of inroads from Reform UK. Notwithstanding Conservative efforts to regain Reform voters by taking a tougher line on immigration, a YouGov December 2025 survey reported that the party had lost to Reform 28 per cent of those who had voted Tory at the 2024 election. Given the extent to which the Conservative Party has moved away from the centre, it had little support to lose to the three parties on the left.

Demography is slowly eroding the Conservative vote, as its older supporters are dying off and younger voters are not replacing them. At the last general election, the Conservatives did best among voters age 75 or older, getting 46 per cent of the group's vote as against 20 per cent going to Labour. That support is contracting annually as mortality takes its toll of elderly voters. At the next election the electorate will be replenished by young people voting for the first time and their number will be boosted by the Labour government's plan to lower the voting age to 16. At the 2024 general election, the Tories won only 8 per cent of the under-25 vote, while Labour won five times as much. By December 2025 they were in fifth place in the competition for the vote of young people.

The bulk of Conservative defectors who have shifted their support to Reform UK do not see this as due to a big change in their political views. They simply see Nigel Farage as advocating tougher action against illegal immigrants and as a more effective opponent of Labour than Kemi Badenoch. They also view the last Conservative government as lacking competence and confused in what it was doing. Only 26 per cent of Tory defectors say they would never vote Conservative again, according to an October 2025 Lord Ashcroft Poll, while 24 per cent say that if the party got its act together after losing the last election they might vote for it at the next election. The largest group, 43 per cent, say they might one day vote Conservative again but probably not at the next election.

Invoking political values avoids getting bogged down in debates about which party is to blame for Britain's current problems. However, there is a problem with this approach: the groups with the most pro-Conservative values are limited in size. Of six value clusters identified by the British Social Attitudes survey (see chapter 3.4), only Well-Off Traditionalists are strongly in favour of the Conservative Party. However, they are only one-eighth of the electorate and the Conservatives must compete with Reform for their support. Left-Behind Patriots share anti-woke values with Conservatives, but are more likely to struggle financially. Thus, that group's party preferences divide almost equally between left-of-centre and right-of-centre parties.

The 2025 Conservative Party conference gave party leaders the chance to champion policy proposals aimed at attracting Reform supporters as well as stopping the further loss of its core supporters. To deal with immigration, Kemi Badenoch promised that a Conservative government would withdraw from the European Convention on Human Rights, which British judges sometimes cite when ruling in favour of illegal and legal immigrants. Badenoch said that repeal would mean 'We can run government for the people of this country, not for everybody else who shows up'. To symbolise its anti-immigrant commitment, the party has introduced in Parliament a bill that would put a statutory cap on the annual number of immigrants and authorise the deportation of legal as well as illegal immigrants.

Wielding a judge's wig, the former Cabinet minister Robert Jenrick has attacked activist judges favouring immigrants by making decisions based on their sympathy with pro-immigrant organisations. He claimed this was undermining public trust in the law. To stop this practice, Jenrick said that, if the Conservatives controlled government, Cabinet ministers would take a bigger hand in vetting and appointing judges.

In a bid to promote the Conservatives' image as a pro-market, low-tax party, the shadow chancellor, Mel Stride, told the party conference that it would reduce public expenditure by £47 billion by cutting welfare spending and the size of the civil service, both of which had grown under the previous Conservative government. In addition there was a pledge to scrap stamp duty that buyers must pay when buying a house. A shadow minister described the 2025 party conference as 'competent', by contrast with the party's behaviour in its previous term in government: 'We didn't fight like ferrets in a sack' (Parker et al., 2025).

When YouGov tested the standing of the parties immediately after party conferences, it found the Conservatives were still in third place with the support of 17 per cent of voters. This put the party closer to the two parties tied for fourth place at 15 per cent, the Liberal Democrats and Greens, than to the second-place Labour Party. Reform was in the lead, as has consistently been the case since spring 2025. Moreover, Reform was thought to be better at handling immigration and the economy than the Conservatives.

Changing leaders?

Changing the leader is something that a party can do when it is in the doldrums, and it is much more easily done than changing the electorate, albeit empirical research suggests that changing leaders has little effect compared to changing the party's performance on issues. Conservative MPs have frequently ditched party leaders who were not attracting votes. After going into opposition in 1997, the party had four leaders – William Hague, Iain Duncan Smith, Michael Howard and David Cameron – before winning the 2010 general election. In the 14 years of Conservative government that followed, more of the party's prime ministers left office when they lost the confidence of Tory MPs than those who left due to electoral defeat.

The rules of the Conservative Party make it relatively easy to call a leadership contest; only 15 per cent of the party's MPs need to sign a petition to call a ballot, and a candidate needs only ten MP's signatures to be nominated. If more than two candidates are nominated, MPs vote in a series of ballots, with the bottom candidate in each round eliminated. The top two candidates then go forward to a vote of the party's membership. To become party leader requires the endorsement of fewer than 1 per cent of Conservative voters and a few hundredths of 1 per cent of the electorate (cf. Figure 2.1). The requirement for a candidate to be a sitting MP is an obstacle to Boris Johnson contesting the leadership unless he were to fight and win a by-election before a leadership contest was called.

Of the three leaders competing to become prime minister today, Kemi Badenoch has the lowest public profile. In YouGov's survey of the favourability of party leaders in November 2025, there were 22 per cent having no opinion of her. By contrast, only 10 per cent had no opinion of Keir Starmer. The 26 per cent who reported a favourable opinion of Badenoch were fewer than the 29 per cent favourably disposed to Farage, but 8 percentage points higher than those favourable towards Keir Starmer.

Kemi Badenoch's inability to reverse the party's loss of electoral support has encouraged speculation among Tory MPs about getting a new party leader. The leadership candidate she defeated, Robert Jenrick, ran a social media campaign with stunts highlighting failures in Labour's dealings with illegal immigrants and petty criminals. Since the 2025 party conference Badenoch's performance in grilling the prime minister in parliamentary questions and the party edging up even to Labour in the polls has quelled talk of her replacement for the time being, and Jenrick's defection to Reform UK has removed her chief challenger. The outcome of local and devolved government elections in May 2026 will provide ballot-box evidence of the party's standing with the electorate.

Linking with Reform?

The current political situation offers the Conservatives another alternative route back to government: make a deal with Reform UK. The arithmetic logic is simple. The Labour Party has demonstrated that in a six-party system of competition a parliamentary majority can be gained with little more than one-third of the popular vote, thanks to the mechanics of the first-past-the-post system. At the 2024 election the two right-wing parties between them won fewer than one-fifth of the seats in the House of Commons because they divided 38.0 per cent of the popular vote. By autumn 2025 the combined poll support of the two parties was above 45 per cent. However, some party loyalists would refuse to vote for an alliance of the Conservatives and Reform.

The political logic of a right-wing alliance is complicated. Whereas at the 2024 election the Conservatives had by far the bigger share of votes and seats of the two parties, the position is now reversed. Reform UK is leading the Conservative Party by a big margin in both poll support and projected seats (see Table 9.1 and Appendix Table 3). Nigel Farage has stated that the object of Reform UK is not to work with the Conservative Party but to supplant it as one of Britain's two governing parties. Moreover, he is distrustful of Conservatives after being misled by Boris Johnson when Brexit Party candidates stood down to help the Conservatives win seats at the 2019 general election. For any Conservative leader, doing a deal with Reform UK from a position of weakness would demote the Tory leader to being an ornamental deputy leader in which all eyes were fixed on Nigel Farage. It would also threaten the disappearance of the Conservative Party in a much larger Reform UK party.

Conservatives at the grass-roots are already beginning to join forces with Reform UK. Voters see no major obstacle in terms of policy goals. In the case of immigration and asylum, Reform's claim that it will be more effective than the last Conservative government has not been tested and failed. Moreover, the Labour government's tax-raising measures and anti-business policies have made getting rid of the Labour government the overriding priority of right-wing voters. As long as Nigel

Farage's party is perceived as more likely to do this than the Conservatives, it would be wasting a vote to return to the Conservative fold.

Conservative politicians are also starting to evaluate the electoral attraction of joining with Reform UK. There is now a cohort of former Conservative MPs who lost their seats to Labour at the 2024 general election and have joined Reform. Doing so offers ex-MPs a potential route back to the House of Commons by regaining their seats from Labour with Reform support added to any personal following they had accumulated there. To a party short of experienced politicians, this would add parliamentary and sometimes ministerial experience that Reform UK lacks.

Critical decisions about joining forces do not need to be taken until 2029. If Reform UK's support has slumped significantly in the polls and Conservative support has risen, then an alliance modelled on the SDP–Liberal pact in 1983 could be mooted, with the two parties agreeing not to fight each other at the constituency level. This would make incumbent Tory MPs electorally secure and leave it up to Reform to contest and win hundreds of seats from an unpopular Labour government. If the two parties competed against each other at the constituency level, it would then be up to the first-past-the-post electoral system to decide which of the two parties or Labour came out best.

If an election were held with the division of the vote the same as at the start of 2026, Reform UK would be the big winner (see chapter 9). But it would not necessarily win enough seats to form a government on its own. In that case the Conservatives would be in a position to join Reform UK in a coalition government in which its MPs with ministerial experience could command major posts. The alternative would be to withhold support and face a second election in which a minority Reform government would seek to win a majority that would wipe out the Conservative Party.

There is no need for the Conservatives to start debating in 2026 what they would do if faced with hypothetical challenges in three years' time. Changing the leadership of the Conservative Party is a simple, ready-at-hand change that the party can make. However, whoever is the leader will face the challenge of crafting a clear and simple appeal that puts its failings in government behind it. Even if this has little effect, it buys time until something better turns up that is out of its control, for example Reform UK losing electoral support with the same rocket-like speed that it has attracted voters.

Citations

Difford, Dylan, 2025a. 'How would Britain vote, a year since the 2024 election', https://yougov.co.uk/politics/articles/52431-how-would-britain-vote-a-year-since-the-2024-election. Accessed 21 December 2025.

Difford, Dylan, 2025b. 'Which parties are best at handling the key issues?', https://yougov.co.uk/politics/articles/52447-which-parties-are-best-at-handling-the-key-issues-june-2025. Accessed 21 December 2025.

Parker, George, Sheppard, D., Fleming, S. and Strauss, D., 2025. 'Badenoch makes £9bn pledge to scrap stamp duty', *Financial Times*, 9 October.

Rayson, Steve, 2024. *Collapse of the Conservatives*. Midhurst: Bavant Press.

7

Reform UK: Institutionalising charisma?

The term charisma is derived from an ancient Greek word referring to the gift of grace from the gods; it was assimilated into Christian theology to refer to the divine character of major biblical persons. The German sociologist Max Weber (1947: 64ff) then used the term to describe a leader with a personal appeal so strong that their followers unquestioningly accepted the leader's authority. A charismatic leader uses their authority to disrupt established institutions of society. If this is achieved, the leader then faces the challenge of institutionalising their charisma in a new and durable regime.

Both Adolf Hitler and Charles de Gaulle were charismatic leaders in the first sense, disrupting political regimes. Hitler used his personal authority to disrupt Germany's Weimar Republic and replace it with the Third Reich. It was meant to last one thousand years, but perished with him after twelve years. De Gaulle showed charismatic authority by establishing a Provisional Government of the French Republic in exile during the Second World War. After France regained sovereignty, de Gaulle failed to institutionalise his desired presidential authority and retired rather than participate in the politics of the Fourth French Republic. When that republic collapsed, de Gaulle met both tests of charismatic leadership. He established a powerful presidency, the Fifth French Republic, and it has endured and may soon become the country's longest-lasting regime since the French Revolution.

The term charismatic is often applied in British political discourse to describe almost any politician who becomes prime minister, whatever their personality. David Lloyd George, a speaker of great appeal, met the first test of being a charismatic leader, heading a wartime coalition government that caused the Liberal Party to lose its status as a party of government. He failed the second test; the party he established was simply a vehicle to deliver seats in the Commons for his family rather than seats in Cabinet. Winston Churchill is often referred to as a charismatic leader, but he spent decades excluded from government until heading a wartime coalition to defend Britain's established system of government. The ups and downs in every prime minister's popularity show that it is their performance in office rather than their personality that is most important for their electoral success (see Table 2.1).

In the course of establishing himself as a major force in British politics, Nigel Farage has belonged to four different political parties. He left the Conservatives when the party backed the Maastricht Treaty that created the European Union in 1992. Farage was a founding member of the United Kingdom Independence Party (UKIP). His big breakthrough was when pressure from

UKIP led Prime Minister David Cameron to call and lose a referendum on EU membership. Farage then retired as UKIP leader and, when that party drifted to the far right, Farage created the Brexit Party to campaign for EU withdrawal without conditions. Once Brexit was accomplished, the party morphed into Reform UK under Farage's leadership.

For the greater part of his career, the governing parties treated Nigel Farage as a populist outsider. A close adviser of David Cameron called Farage and his followers 'mad, swivel-eyed loons'. The general secretary of the Trades Union Congress described him as a 'political fraud'. In 2023 Coutts, a prestigious private bank, cancelled Farage's account, describing him in an internal memorandum as a 'xenophobe, pandering to racists, and disingenuous grifter'.

The 2024 general election, the first that Reform UK contested, was a turning point politically. Nigel Farage finally won a seat in the House of Commons, and Reform UK finished third in votes though it tied for sixth in seats. Farage has positioned Reform as the chief alternative to the failings of what he calls the uniparty, that is, the Labour and Conservative Parties that have long governed Britain. This anti-establishment strategy, abetted by the shortcomings of the Labour government, has taken Reform UK to first place in the opinion polls in the first year of the current Parliament (see Appendix Table 3).

The first section of this chapter shows how Farage has gone from winning attention to winning votes. The second documents how Reform has been transformed from a private company literally owned by Farage into a party organised to contest elections nationwide. The concluding section sets out the challenges that Reform faces in its efforts to transform itself from a protest party into a potential party of government.

From winning attention to winning votes

Two anti-EU parties were created in reaction to the Conservative government approving the Maastricht Treaty turning the European Economic Community into the European Union with enhanced powers. A London School of Economics lecturer, Alan Sked, turned the Anti-Federalist League into the United Kingdom Independence Party. Sir James Goldsmith founded the single-issue Referendum Party to campaign for a popular vote on whether the United Kingdom should leave the EU. At the 1997 British general election the Referendum Party fielded 547 candidates, but won only 2.6 per cent of the national vote. UKIP won only three-tenths of 1 per cent of the national vote, and 192 of its 193 candidates lost their deposit. Nigel Farage was the exception. When Goldsmith died shortly after the election, the Referendum Party was dissolved, leaving UKIP the only anti-EU party in the field.

UKIP gained little benefit by nominating more candidates. In 2001 it fought a majority of seats for the first time, but got only 1.5 per cent of the national vote and lost 422 of its 428 deposits. In 2005 it nominated more candidates and won 2.2 per cent of the national vote. UKIP reached 3.1 per cent of the national vote in 2010, and 99 of its 558 candidates saved their deposit by securing more than 5 per cent of their constituency's vote. The focus on the EU gave impetus to UKIP. In 2015 it won 3.8 million votes, 12.6 per cent of the national total, and saved its deposit in seven-eighths of the 624 seats the party fought. This pushed the Liberal Democrats into fourth place in terms of votes. However, UKIP again finished bottom in the competition for MPs. Because its votes were spread relatively evenly nationwide, UKIP was unable to win a single seat.

Ironically, the mandating of proportional representation for elections to the European Parliament (EP) gave UKIP a chance to offset its futile efforts to win first-past-the-post seats in the House of Commons with successfully gaining seats in the EP. Opponents of the EU were more likely to vote and, as turnout was less than half that in a general election, this doubled the weight of their vote. In 1999 UKIP won 6.5 per cent of the vote and three of Britain's 87 EP seats. Its vote and seats grew to a peak in the low-turnout vote in 2014: 27 per cent and 24 seats. In addition, the EP provided UKIP with generous salaries and money for expenses and party organisation. Nigel Farage was a member of the European Parliament for 21 years.

The 2016 referendum made UKIP's main issue the centre of attention. However, the role of the party was diminished because party names were not on the ballot. The Electoral Commission funded Vote Leave as the official cross-party organisation campaigning for Brexit.

Nigel Farage was the leading figure in Grassroots Out, which campaigned for Brexit and argued with Vote Leave about campaign tactics and personalities.

The majority vote to leave the EU was more than four times the vote that UKIP had got at the general election a year before. Nigel Farage resigned as leader of UKIP, mission accomplished. Responsibility for delivering Brexit was in the hands of the Conservative government and a Parliament in which both the government and opposition MPs were split. UKIP fought the 2017 election and won only 1.8 per cent of the national vote. The next year Farage resigned from UKIP when it established links with the racist British National Party.

To keep his political options open, in November 2018 Nigel Farage registered The Brexit Party Ltd as a private company to campaign for leaving the EU without any concessions to Brussels. When the 2019 election was called, Farage offered an electoral pact to Boris Johnson, who rejected the offer. The Brexit Party nominated 275 candidates, most of whom were in seats that did not have a Conservative MP. It won only 2.0 per cent of the vote, and three-fifths of its candidates lost their deposit. UKIP nominated 44 candidates, all of whom lost their deposit. Farage was not a candidate.

Reform UK: an anti-party party

Nigel Farage saw that getting Brexit done made UKIP, a single-issue party, redundant. He re-registered his privately owned Brexit Party as the Reform UK Party.

Farage owned 53 per cent of the shares and named himself Honorary President of the organisation. He engaged in profitable media work and cultivated contacts with Donald Trump's entourage in Washington rather than campaign against a Johnson-led Conservative government that appeared solidly entrenched (Crick, 2022). Richard Tice, a co-owner of the party, became Reform UK's leader.

Reform UK gained support by broadening engagement with issues. During the Covid crisis Reform campaigned against extended lockdowns of public facilities. It also called for a reduction in taxes. It argued for strict control of immigration, a subject both governing parties chose to avoid. The collapse of popular support for the Conservative government gave Reform an MP when Lee Anderson, a Conservative MP and an ex-Labour councillor, defected. Opponents sought to stigmatise Reform as an extremist populist party. However, when populist parties began winning votes across Europe from unpopular governing parties, this became an ambiguous tribute.

Nigel Farage has also sought to narrow the choice of government to two parties, Reform UK and a 'uniparty' consisting of Conservative and Labour governments that followed the same establishment agenda in favour of multi-culturalism, 'woke' policies on things such as gender relations and Europe. Electoral Calculus and Find Out Now (2025) conducted a split-sample survey of the general public and of individuals belonging to a broadly defined establishment class of lecturers, legal and medical professionals and security personnel. The views of establishment respondents differed significantly from those of the general public. In the establishment group, 75 per cent favoured the three left-of-centre parties, half again more than the general public. Among those categorised as lecturers – academics, media and cultural workers and school teachers – more than four-fifths favoured left parties and endorsed political opinions similar to the views of Labour voters. However, in the security establishment of military and police personnel, 49 per cent favoured parties of the right against more than 43 per cent favouring Labour or the Liberal Democrats.

Disrupting the competition for votes and seats

Reform was an invisible party in the opinion polls at the start of the 2019–24 Parliament. Many polls did not offer respondents Reform in their list of parties or still referred to the Brexit Party. When YouGov started reporting support for Reform in March 2020, it had only 2 per cent support. This put it in sixth place, behind not only the two governing parties but also the Liberal Democrats, the Scottish National Party and the Green Party. By the end of that year Reform had reached 5 per cent support, a critical level for saving constituency deposits but not for winning seats in the House of Commons. In September 2021 Reform first registered 10 per cent in opinion polls. Once Labour captured the lead in the polls, support for UKIP fell as low as 5 per cent. Boris Johnson's 'Partygate' scandal and Liz Truss's brief and economically disastrous premiership gave Reform a boost. At the end of 2023 Reform's support had reached 11 per cent. As a general election loomed, Reform picked up more support, reaching 16 per cent in early April 2024.

When Conservative Prime Minister Rishi Sunak called an early election in late spring 2024, Nigel Farage belatedly decided to stand again. In a nod to the electoral majority that had voted for Brexit eight years earlier, Farage pledged to 'take back control over our borders, our money and our laws'. Reform's party-political television slot on 13 June showed its slogan in silence: 'Britain is Broken. Britain Needs Reform.'

Like the Labour Party, Reform's manifesto pledged change, but in a different direction. It endorsed the introduction of a British Bill of Rights to replace the European Convention on Human Rights and making St George's Day a public holiday. The manifesto highlighted five core pledges: curbing non-essential and illegal immigration; cutting income tax; abandoning net zero energy policies; boosting the earnings of lower-paid workers; and eliminating NHS waiting lists. The manifesto claimed that its spending would be met by cutting wasteful expenditure and boosting economic growth, an approach that Labour also touted.

Immigration was the most important issue in the minds of Reform voters; it was mentioned by 82 per cent of the party's supporters (cf. Table 5.1). By contrast, only 10 per cent of Labour voters and 45 per cent of Conservative voters cited it as one of the three most important issues in the election. Reform supporters were also more than twice as likely to be concerned with crime, 23 per cent, than were supporters of other parties. While one-third of Reform voters named the cost of living as important, this number was substantially lower than the economic concerns of supporters for other parties. By contrast with the 2019 election, relations with the European Union were of little interest; they were cited as important by only 5 per cent of Reform voters.

The outcome of the general election gave Reform UK 4.1 million votes, 14.3 per cent of the national total, and 577 of its candidates saved their deposits. The four-million-plus voters who backed the party were too numerous to be dismissed as swivel-eyed loons. However, the first-past-the-post electoral system gave Reform only five MPs, including a seat for Nigel Farage.

Reform UK gained three-quarters of its votes from Conservatives who were dissatisfied with how the party had mismanaged policies in government, as well as not being Conservative enough. This gave Reform the impetus it needed to overtake the Liberal Democrats in national votes; it also deprived the Conservatives of one-quarter of their 2019 support according to a massive post-election YouGov poll. Thus, while Reform won only five MPs, it won enough Tory votes to cost the Conservatives control of government.

With few MPs to lead in the Commons, Nigel Farage can give priority to exploiting the party's appeal through old and new media. He does this by frequent media briefings and well-publicised appearances in constituencies that are potentially winnable for Reform and in pubs. While media coverage of the Labour government and the Conservatives tends to focus on their loss of support and internal difficulties, stories about Reform UK focus on its success in winning votes by offering an alternative to the two parties.

The number of followers Farage has for his X accounts, 2.2 million, is greater than the number of followers of Prime Minister Keir Starmer. Furthermore, Farage now has as many followers on TikTok as all other MPs combined. Reform UK's official party site on TikTok similarly leads the accounts of other parties, and Farage's 1.3 million followers on TikTok reach a younger audience. Videos with titles such as 'Isn't it about time we started looking after our own people?' have attracted up to five million viewers (Boyd, Goodier and Courea, 2025; Mason, 2025).

Unseating the governing parties

Coming third in votes in the 2024 election made Reform UK relevant as a competitor for votes. However, with only five MPs it has little influence in Parliament. To become institutionalised as a potential governing party, it needs to win enough MPs to be relevant to the calculation of a parliamentary majority (see chapter 9). This requires it to have a nationwide organisation with lots of constituency candidates who not only save their deposits but also win their seats. This depends upon neither governing party recovering the support it has lost in the current Parliament.

Nigel Farage has taken major steps to institutionalise his charisma. In February 2025 he transferred ownership of the party to Reform 2025 Ltd, a non-profit organisation with no shareholders and Farage and Reform's chair, the multi-millionaire businessman Zia Yusuf, as directors. The party began recruiting members via its website. As of December 2025 its membership is more than double that of the Conservative Party and is approaching the Labour Party's membership in more than four hundred branches spread across Britain. New members include well over a dozen ex-Conservative MPs who lost their seats at the 2024 general election. Growing pains have also arisen. Rupert Lowe, one of its five newly elected MPs, was suspended after disputes on policy and personality and left the party. In the second half of 2025, its finances received an enormous boost when Christopher Harbone, a technology investor and former donor to the Conservatives, pledged a donation of £9 million.

Gaining more support

Nigel Farage has expanded Reform's vote by claiming it is the 'true voice of the ordinary working man and woman' and endorsing soft-left policies such as the nationalisation of the British steel industry and an end to the two-child cap on child benefits. A steady flow of opinion polls in the new Parliament soon showed Reform UK becoming a major runner in a three-horse race with the two governing parties. In the December 2024 monthly average of polls, Reform support went above 20 per cent for the first time. Since April 2025 Reform has been first in the monthly average of opinion polls. In December 2025 Reform led with the support of 28 per cent of poll respondents, giving it an 8 percentage point lead over Labour (see Appendix Table 3).

The doubling of Reform's support has been accompanied by attracting voters from the parties on the left as well as from the Conservatives on the right. To reach 30 per cent in the polls it has doubled its vote at the last election, which came disproportionately from disaffected Tories. Three-fifths of its new recruits have come from additional Conservative defectors while more than one-third come from those who had voted in 2024 for left-of-centre parties, the Liberal Democrats, Labour and the Greens. Among working-class voters, Reform now has a 14 percentage point lead over Labour, while Labour has a statistically insignificant 1 point lead over Reform among middle-class voters. Education is the biggest social divide; voters with less formal education tend to favour Reform UK while those with higher education favour Labour.

A majority of the electorate has a negative view of Reform UK. An average of December 2025 polls finds that 46 per cent have an unfavourable view of the party, compared to 26 per cent being favourable. This gives it a net unfavourable rating of minus 20 per cent. Comparatively speaking, this is not a handicap. Consistent with the disruption of the party system, even more people have a negative view of the Labour and Conservative Parties.

Local council elections in England in May 2025 provided the first ballot-box test of Reform's support in this Parliament. Reform showed that it was more than a one-man band or an internet phenomenon by nominating more candidates than either the Labour or Conservative Parties. It won 677 council seats and gained control of ten councils from traditionally Conservative Kent to traditionally Labour Durham. The Conservative Party lost 675 council seats and control of 16 councils. Labour was defending far fewer council seats but nevertheless lost two-thirds of the seats it was defending (Buchanan, Stiebahl and Wong, 2025). Local election psephologists Colin Rallings and Michael Thrasher (2025) projected that, if the local election result was repeated at a parliamentary election, Reform UK would take 32 per cent of the national vote and finish 13 percentage points ahead of Labour.

While Labour could publicly dismiss bad local election results as a poor guide to Westminster, it could not dismiss as irrelevant the loss of one of its notionally safest seats, Runcorn & Helsby, to Reform UK in a by-election held the same day as the 2025 local elections. At the general election ten months before, Labour had won Runcorn with an absolute majority and a 35 percentage point lead over Reform.

Even though the majority of people registering support for Reform UK today have yet to cast a vote for the party at a general election, they cannot be described as weakly committed floating voters. A Lord Ashcroft Poll in August 2025 found that five-sixths of Reform voters are definitely committed to voting for the party at the next general election. This is half again more than the proportion of committed Labour supporters.

The millions of Britons backing Reform are now too numerous for the governing parties to dismiss. Days after Reform's local election breakthrough, Keir Starmer began attacking Reform as 'the real opposition' on the grounds that the Conservative Party was in hopeless decline. At the Labour Party's annual conference, the prime minister described Farage as a 'snake oil merchant' peddling dangerous medicines. Labour, on the initiative of Home Secretary Shabana Mahmood, has sought to win back support from anti-immigration voters attracted to Reform by announcing plans to cut immigration and promptly deport illegal immigrants. However, only 4 per cent of Reform voters say they would consider voting Labour, compared to 79 per cent saying they would never consider voting Labour (Difford, 2025).

Increased popular support has stimulated journalists and partisan opponents to find stories that could discredit Nigel Farage personally as well as his party. For example, in autumn 2025 *The Guardian* ran stories reporting antisemitic and racist remarks that Farage is said to have made to fellow teenage students at Dulwich College. Farage dismissed the remarks as youthful banter common in the 1970s, like the BBC's popular *Black and White Minstrel Show*. A former Reform councillor in dispute with Farage gave police a file alleged to contain evidence showing that Farage had violated the election expenses law when winning his Clacton seat in 2024. The struggles that newly elected and inexperienced Reform councillors are having to meet their election pledges on such things as tax and spending cuts provide a continuing flow of stories for local and occasionally national media.

Could Reform UK go all the way?

The general election of 2029 is more than three years away. Hundreds of polls are still to be taken, and by-elections will give a small number of voters the chance to express their views in constituencies selected by accident. Multi-level regression with post-stratification (MRP) predictions of the Reform MPs show that a few percentage points difference in the popular vote can make a critical difference between winning an absolute majority or merely a plurality of seats in the House of Commons (see Table 9.1). In December 2024, when Reform was averaging almost 22 per cent in the polls, an MRP projection showed the first-past-the-post system working against Reform, giving it only 75 seats. By Easter 2025, when Reform was first in the polls with an average of 25 per cent of the vote, its predicted seat share had risen to 175 MPs, virtually the same as its share of the popular vote. By autumn 2025 Reform was benefiting from the first-past-the-post system. With its support averaging 30 per cent in the polls, half of MRP analyses predicted it would win an absolute majority of seats in Parliament and the other half predicted it would come first with upwards of three hundred seats.

We can already identify known facts and known unknowns that will affect Reform's position once the 2029 general election is held. If Reform UK is to become a major party after the next election, in order to become the largest party it must add well over two hundred seats to the five it won at the 2024 general election. Winning 150 or more seats would probably deprive both the Labour and Conservative Parties of winning control of government with a parliamentary majority.

Although Reform takes lots of votes from the Conservatives, it cannot win all the seats it needs from that party because the Conservatives have only 121 MPs and Reform is second to the Tories in only nine seats. Even if Reform were to take all of the Conservative Party's constituencies, it would remain a weak opposition party in the House of Commons.

There are some 130 constituencies in which the combined vote for the Reform and Conservative Parties is greater than 50 per cent and an additional 140 seats where it is greater than that of any other party. In theory, if the two parties were to agree an electoral pact about nominating a single candidate in each constituency and their supporters voted as a bloc to support the pact's nominee, this could produce enough MPs to form a government. However, such an assumption is not politically viable. Nigel Farage has made clear that Reform's aim is not to create a right-wing coalition but to destroy the Conservatives and become a party that governs on its own.

If Reform UK is to become the leading party in the next House of Commons it must take more than 150 seats from Labour to add to whatever it takes from the Conservatives. At the last general election Reform finished second to Labour in 89 constituencies. As long as Labour voters are dissatisfied with the performance of the Starmer government, Reform indirectly gains from defectors to other left-of-centre parties reducing Labour's constituency lead over it and gains even more from the limited number of Labour voters who defect to Reform.

Reform UK's leading position in the polls has the potential to stimulate tactical voting to keep Reform from taking control of government. When opinion polls ask respondents to evaluate party leaders, up to one-third rate Nigel Farage positively. This is sufficient to make him the most popular party leader, since other leaders have even lower ratings. Up to half express a negative view of Farage. However, this does not make him Britain's most unpopular leader because Keir Starmer is viewed negatively by two-thirds to three-quarters of respondents (Wikipedia, 2025). Moreover, while more people tend to view Reform negatively than positively, its negative rating tends to be lower than that for either the Labour or Conservative Parties.

It is politically impossible for the leaders of Labour or the Conservatives to encourage their supporters to vote tactically for the other governing party on the grounds it is the lesser evil than Reform, a party that has yet to be seen to misgovern Britain. In a contest in which voters are free to choose (see chapter 3), tactical voting does not require public endorsement by party leaders. It simply requires voters to have a strong enough dislike of the prospect of a Reform government and knowledge of which party in their constituency has the best chance of defeating Reform UK. If that is not their preferred party, then the stronger their dislike of

Reform, the readier they will be to cast a tactical vote for a second-choice or lesser-evil party in hopes of defeating the Reform candidate.

To estimate the potential impact of tactical voting, Electoral Calculus (2025) has combined survey data about the readiness of individuals to vote tactically with the analysis of the effect of tactical voting at the level of each constituency, as there are big differences between constituencies in which party is best placed to win it (see Table 4.3). When asked how they would vote in a contest in which Reform and the Conservatives were the two parties with the best chance of winning the seat, 38 per cent of Labour voters said they would vote tactically for the Tories, and Liberal Democrat and Green supporters responded similarly. When asked about voting in a constituency in which Labour and Reform were the chief contenders, 52 per cent of Conservatives said they would vote for Reform compared to 11 per cent favouring Labour. By contrast, a large number of Liberal Democrats and Green supporters would tend to vote Labour.

A projection of the effect of tactical voting on seats in the House of Commons assumes that voters have an accurate perception of the state of party competition not only in national polls but also in their constituency. Setting aside this qualification, Electoral Calculus reckons that Reform would fail to win up to 67 seats if all electors cast tactical ballots to the extent that polls have suggested. This would be enough to save 42 Labour MPs from losing their seats because of the unpopularity of the Starmer government. Thus, Reform would be left to form a minority government two dozen short of a majority. This would still leave it more than 125 seats ahead of Labour.

If the Labour government's lack of popularity continues, this could create the conditions for tactical voting benefiting Reform UK as the party best placed to turn it out of office. The 341 seats that Labour won with less than half the vote are particularly vulnerable to tactical voting. Even though the Conservatives finished second in most of these seats at the 2024 election, Reform's well-publicised lead in the polls may help it be seen as the best bet by tactical voters who want to oust a Labour government at any cost.

The important question in Whitehall is: how could Nigel Farage fill up to a hundred ministerial posts? The answer is: with some difficulty. More than 95 per cent of Reform MPs would be new to Parliament and unfamiliar with Whitehall ministries. Farage has said he would recruit talented people from outside the Westminster bubble. Even if businesspeople were given a peerage and sat in the House of Lords, they would have to answer to lords with lots of ministerial experience and incentives to test the new appointees' knowledge of the business of politics. If parliamentary accountability is to be maintained, a novice MP in the role of a junior minister would have to answer for the department in the House of Commons.

The only way in which Nigel Farage could form a Cabinet with experienced ministers is by appointing ex-Conservative ministers. By the end of January 2026 three former Conservative ministers, Robert Jenrick,

Nadhim Zahawi, Robert Jenrick and Suella Braverman, had resigned from the Tory Party and joined Reform UK.

Citations

Boyd, Raphael, Goodier, Michael and Courea, Eleni, 2025. 'Nigel Farage is a hit on TikTok', *The Guardian*, 12 May.

Buchanan, Isobel, Stiebahl, S. and Wong, H., 2025. *Local Elections 2025: Results and Analysis*. London: House of Commons Library Research Briefing.

Crick, Michael, 2022. *One Party After Another: The Disruptive Life of Nigel Farage*. London: Simon & Schuster.

Difford, Dylan, 2025. 'Britons think Labour is going after Reform voters – but are they interested?', https://yougov.co.uk/politics/articles/52221-britons-think-labour-is-going-after-reform-uk-voters-but-are-they-interested. Accessed 21 December 2025.

Electoral Calculus, 2025. 'Tactical voting 2025', www.electoralcalculus.co.uk/blogs/pseph_tactical_2025.html. Accessed 21 December 2025.

Find Out Now, 2025. 'Establishment Poll 2025', https://www.electoralcalculus.co.uk/blogs/ec_estpoll_20251010.html. Accessed 21 December 2025.

Mason, Rowena, 2025. 'Big pay days and top of the polls: Nigel Farage's first year as an MP', *The Guardian*, 6 July.

Rallings, Colin and Thrasher, Michael, 2025. 'How Reform delivered shock to two-party system', *Local Government Chronicle*, 7 May.

Swinford, Steven, 2025. 'Downbeat Jenrick could be coaxed to defect, Farage told', *The Times*, 4 December.

Weber, Max, 1947. *The Theory of Social and Economic Organization*. Glencoe, IL: Free Press, translated by A. M. Henderson and Talcott Parsons.

Wikipedia, 2025. 'Leadership approval opinion polling', https://en.wikipedia.org/wiki/Leadership_approval_opinion_polling_for_the_next_United_Kingdom_general_election. Accessed 21 December 2025.

8

Four more parties relevant too

The 2024 election turned non-governing parties into fourth-force parties as Reform UK expanded the number of potential governing parties to three. Collectively, fourth-force parties won 28.4 per cent of the vote at the 2024 general election, and ten parties divided 113 seats in the House of Commons. The Liberal Democrats and Greens contested seats throughout Great Britain. The Scottish National Party (SNP), Plaid Cymru and Northern Ireland parties fought constituencies within their nation. Pro-Gaza independent candidates fought Midlands constituencies with many Muslim voters. The great majority of fourth-force candidates saved their deposits.

Each fourth-force party has a ceiling on the number of MPs it can hope to elect. It is fixed for nationalist parties by the allocation of seats to the area of the United Kingdom that they contest. Scotland has 57 seats; Wales 32 seats; and Northern Ireland 18 constituencies. The Liberal Democrats concentrate their campaign resources on upwards of a hundred winnable seats. In 2024 this strategy produced 72 MPs and resulted in 229 lost deposits. The Greens' concern with the environment is relevant nationwide, but combined with a low national vote this results in it winning less than 5 per cent of the vote in 258 seats. Until the Green Party wins a lot more than four MPs, its impact on Parliament will be due to the seats it costs Labour by attracting its voters.

The relevance of a fourth-force seat to the control of government depends on how many seats are won by the party finishing first. While the Labour or Conservative Party has usually governed with an absolute majority of MPs, in two elections since 2010 no party won a majority and the governing party had to depend on a fourth party for a parliamentary majority. In 2010 David Cameron became the Conservative prime minister thanks to a coalition pact that gave the Liberal Democrats seats in Cabinet in exchange for it contributing the MPs that gave the coalition its parliamentary majority. When Theresa May fell a few seats short of a parliamentary majority in 2017, she relied on the Northern Ireland Democratic Unionist Party's nine MPs to maintain her place in Downing Street. By contrast, in 2024 the Liberal Democrats' 72 MPs were of no account to government because Labour won a massive parliamentary majority.

The following pages detail the different ways in which fourth-force parties fit into the jigsaw-puzzle composition of the House of Commons. Even though they do not alternate in control of government, they may influence whatever government is formed if a general election fails to produce a parliamentary majority. What they want differs among parties. The Liberal Democrats would like to influence policy by becoming ministers in a British government. Nationalist parties would like to get independence from British government. As long as they do not have enough MPs to affect a government majority, the Greens may simply influence the policy of governing parties.

Liberal Democrats: a floor and a ceiling

Although a non-governing party, the Liberal Democrats have always presented a programme covering the same range of issues as the two governing parties. When the party's position is the same as that of one or both governing parties, this has limited electoral appeal since a non-governing party cannot put its policies into effect. It campaigns in its target constituencies on consensus goals such as mending potholes in local roads. Its national manifesto opened with the claim, 'Every vote for the Liberal Democrats is a vote to elect a strong local champion who will fight for a fair deal for you and your community.' Although it is historically the most pro-European of British parties, the Liberal Democrats' policies on Europe were buried in the final chapter of its 2024 election manifesto and stopped short of calling for Britain to rejoin the European Union.

The Liberal Democrats' 2024 national vote, 12.2 per cent, was virtually static, just a fraction of 1 percentage point up from its vote in 2019. This left it in fourth place in terms of votes, only the second time in its history it had sunk this low. In 2015 it trailed UKIP, and in 2024 it trailed Reform UK. In both instances, the Lib Dems greatly outnumbered the anti-EU parties in terms of seats won. At the last election the party gained marginally more support from Labour defectors than from Tory defectors. Its supporters divided almost evenly between placing themselves on the left or in the centre; barely one-tenth placed themselves on the right.

In the current Parliament the monthly poll support of the Lib Dems has fluctuated at a slightly higher but statistically insignificant level than its vote at the last election. It was highest in May and July 2025 when 14.1 per cent expressed an intention to vote for the party, and has not been below its general election share of votes since January 2025 (see Appendix Table 3). In December 2025 the surge in Green support pushed the Liberal Democrats down to fifth place.

As a left-of-centre party (see Figure 3.1), the Liberal Democrats offer a near-at-hand choice for Labour voters dissatisfied with the Labour government. However, there are only six constituencies in which a Liberal Democrat candidate finished second to Labour in 2024, thereby being in a position to gain a seat if there is a significant fall in Labour support. Defections from the Conservatives to Reform UK could weaken the Tory hold on 20 seats in which Liberal Democrat candidates are second to a Conservative MP.

The first aim of the Liberal Democrats at the next general election is to retain the 72 seats they won at the 2024 election, almost all from the Tories, thanks to the massive unpopularity of the Conservative government. As long as the Conservatives do not recover, Liberal Democrat MPs are safe from the traditional argument that a vote for them is a wasted vote since the party cannot form a government. There are only two seats where the Lib Dems are second to Labour, thus minimising the seats they could gain from a collapse in Labour support. There is both a high floor and a low ceiling for the number of MPs that the Liberal Democrats can expect to win in the current state of party competition.

If the Liberal Democrats held the balance of power in the next House of Commons, the party would be on the spot. In left–right terms, it is much closer to Labour than to the Conservatives. However, it would hold the balance only if the Labour government was discredited and lost more than one hundred seats. In addition to an ideological barrier, the Liberal Democrats have a reason to avoid forming a coalition government with the Conservatives, as their leader Nick Clegg did in 2010. The consequence was electoral disaster for the Liberal Democrats at the 2015 election.

Greens: a pressure group and a party

The British first-past-the-post electoral system has been a major obstacle to the Green Party winning seats by stressing a single issue. Voters who put the environment above everything else can save a candidate's deposit, but in order for the Greens to win a constituency or even come second there needs to be a substantial concentration of its vote in a limited number of constituencies. Nonetheless, by competing for votes it can put pressure on governing parties to adopt policies to protect the environment. In European countries with proportional representation, green parties have been winning seats in parliament for four decades and sometimes winning Cabinet posts in a coalition government.

British activists were campaigning for government to protect the environment from climate change well before the green movement produced a political party. The Green Party of England and Wales has its origins in the Ecology Party, which nominated 53 candidates at the 1979 general election, all of whom lost their deposits. In 1985 members of the Ecology Party formed the Green Party of the United Kingdom, which won 15 per cent of the vote in the low-turnout 1989 European Parliament election. It then divided into separate national parties, the largest of which is the Green Party of England and Wales. The party began nominating more candidates, winning 1.0 per cent of the national vote for the first time in the 2005 election and returning its first MP in 2010.

The manifesto of the Green Party of England and Wales at the 2024 election dealt with a full range of policies and not just environmental policies and was to the left of the Labour and Liberal Democrat Parties. The manifesto endorsed devolution of power to local groups, the nationalisation of strategic industries, and higher taxes on business and high-income individuals. In foreign policy the Green Party has favoured unilateral nuclear disarmament and the cancellation of debts owed by developing countries, and denounced Israeli actions in Gaza as genocide.

The Green share of the United Kingdom vote jumped to 6.7 per cent in 2024 from 2.7 per cent at the previous election and it saved deposits in 371 of the 629 constituencies it fought. Four Green MPs were elected. More than a quarter of its vote came from supporters of Labour in 2019. This was more than double the support it won from Liberal Democrats and four times that won from defecting Conservatives. Just over half the Green voters were under the age of 25, and university graduates were heavily over-represented. The party finished second to Labour in 40 seats.

In the first 15 months of the current Parliament, the Greens' standing in monthly polls fluctuated at a level 2 percentage points higher than its general election vote. In August 2025 it stood at 8.8 per cent. Zack Polanski won the party leadership in early September with 84 per cent of the party members' vote. He campaigned through social media on a left-wing eco-populist programme that rejected Westminster's emphasis on fiscal constraints and called for the redistribution of wealth to the people left behind. This completed the shift of the Greens from an environmental movement to a party with a broad-based programme to the left of the Starmer government.

The Green Party's left-wing appeal has attracted a fifth of Labour's general election voters disappointed at what they see as a Starmer government more concerned with fiscal rules and competing with Reform UK on immigration than promoting left-wing policies. YouGov surveys show that the Greens are also attracting one-tenth of left-leaning Liberal Democrats, the party that Polanski had previously belonged to. The Greens are the leading party among voters under 25 and draw two-thirds of their support from middle-class voters. As of December 2025 Green support in the polls is averaging 14 per cent. While this places the party in fourth place in electoral support, the widespread distribution of its vote put it sixth in predicted number of MPs (see Table 9.1).

In podcasts Polanski has stressed that the Greens would be open to forming pacts with other left-wing politicians, naming three former Labour MPs, Andy Burnham, Jeremy Corbyn and Zarah Sultana (Wheeler, 2025). A pact would give Green candidates tactical support in dozens of constituencies with concentrations of young and well-educated voters predisposed to the Greens, and in hundreds of constituencies Greens would be mobilised to support other candidates to the left of the Starmer government. However, there is a big political obstacle to a pact: the Greens' best chance of gaining MPs is in the 40 constituencies in which it came second to Labour at the last general election.

Nationalist parties: Westminster elections secondary

Political parties in Scotland, Wales and Northern Ireland compete for seats in their devolved parliament as well as at Westminster. Winning seats in Edinburgh, Cardiff or Belfast is more important than winning seats in the House of Commons. Westminster elections are a means to the end of getting greater powers within their own national parliaments. The Scottish National Party's uncompromising goal is independence. Plaid Cymru wants to create a National Commission to study options for the future of Wales, including the creation of an economically viable and politically independent Welsh state. Northern Ireland parties compete about which nation should govern their land. A variety of unionist parties support keeping the province part of the United Kingdom, while the goal of Sinn Fein is to be part of a united Ireland.

The potential influence of the *Scottish National Party* in Westminster depends on the division of seats between Britain's governing parties. In February 1974 the SNP's seven MPs held the balance of power in a hung parliament with a minority Labour government. Harold Wilson pledged to devolve powers to Scotland in a failed bid to regain Scottish seats; the SNP took 11 seats in the October 1974 election. However, Labour won enough seats in England and Wales to remain in office until 1979. By contrast, in 2019 the SNP won 48 seats without effect at Westminster because the Conservatives won a comfortable majority. The 2016 European Union referendum produced a Scottish majority for remaining in the EU and a majority in England for leaving. The outcome was that the United Kingdom left the EU.

As part of its 2024 sweep of seats throughout Britain, in Scotland Labour took first place from the SNP with 35 per cent of the vote. With six parties competing for votes, the first-past-the-post system gave Labour 37 of Scotland's 57 seats while the SNP's 30 per cent share of the Scottish vote gave it only nine MPs. The reaction against the Conservative government at Westminster was so strong that one-third of Scots who favoured independence voted Labour in order to boot the Tories out. Contrary to the claim that Labour's chances of government depend on Scottish MPs, in 2024 Labour would have won control of government with a comfortable majority even if it had not gained any Scottish seats.

Polls sampling the Scottish electorate during this Parliament have shown two main developments. First of all, the SNP has consistently been the leading party since November 2024. By early December 2025, its support was at 33 per cent in an Ipsos poll, up 3 points from its level at the general election. Secondly, Reform UK has made a breakthrough in Scotland, with 20 per cent support in the Ipsos survey. In parallel with England, Labour support in Scotland has halved since the general election. The Conservatives and Scottish Greens are fighting each other for fourth place. Among polls in this Parliament asking Scots whether they would vote for or against independence in a referendum, ten have shown a majority in favour of independence, six a majority against independence and one a tie.

Plaid Cymru has less potential influence on the outcome of a British election than the SNP. First of all, Wales has only 4.7 per cent of the population of the United Kingdom and 32 seats in the House of Commons. Thus, the 14.8 per cent of the Welsh vote that Plaid won at the 2024 election was less than 0.7 per cent of the total UK vote. Secondly, even at its best Plaid Cymru has never won more than four seats at Westminster, hardly enough to hold the balance of power on its own. For example, in February 1979 Plaid Cymru supported the Labour government in a no confidence vote, but

Labour lost by a single vote because the Liberals and SNP voted no confidence.

Plaid Cymru won its first two seats in the House of Commons in the February 1974 election, which launched the three-party system. Since then it has won up to four seats but has never been relevant in forming a government. At the 2024 general election Plaid Cymru won four seats with 14.8 per cent of the Welsh vote and came second in four constituencies. Labour maximised the benefits of disproportional representation, winning five-sixths of Wales's seats with three-eighths of the vote in the Principality. The Liberal Democrats took one seat while the Conservatives, second in the Welsh vote, did not win any seats. Reform came third with 17 per cent of the vote and likewise failed to win any seats.

In the five Welsh opinion polls taken to date in this Parliament, Labour led in the first two surveys; the third was a tie; and Reform UK has led in the following two. In YouGov's December 2025 poll about Westminster voting intentions, Reform was first with 30 per cent support; Plaid Cymru came second with 19 per cent support; and Labour, with 15 per cent, and the Greens, with 14 per cent, were competing for third place. When voters were asked about their voting intention for the May 2026 election to the devolved Welsh Senedd, there is evidence of multi-level voting, that is individuals supporting different parties depending on whether an election is about representation in the Westminster parliament or in a devolved Senedd. In polls for the Senedd election in 2026 Plaid Cymru comes first with

33 per cent of the vote and Reform UK second with 30 per cent. Labour and the Conservatives compete for third place in the devolved institution, each having 10 per cent support (Larner, 2025).

The death of the Labour member for Caerphilly in the devolved Welsh Senedd created an October 2025 by-election, which showed that Labour's loss of support in Wales was greater than in England. A constituency that had returned Labour MPs for more than a century gave victory to a Plaid Cymru councillor with 47 per cent of the vote on his 14th attempt to win the seat. Reform UK, which had won 20 per cent of the constituency's vote at the Westminster election the year before, increased its support to 36 per cent. Labour's vote was down to 11 per cent, a fall of 27 percentage points from its 2024 Westminster showing.

In *Northern Ireland* elections to its devolved Assembly do not decide which party will govern it. The 1998 Good Friday settlement mandates power-sharing between parties representing the unionist and Irish republican traditions. The party winning the most seats, whichever tradition it belongs to, names the First Minister of the devolved government, while the party representing the other tradition names the Deputy First Minister. If either party refuses to work with the other, no devolved government can be formed; governing the province reverts to the British government in London and this has often happened. The First Minister was the leader of the Democratic Unionist Party until Sinn Fein won the most Assembly seats in 2022 and its leader became First Minister.

In the 2024 Westminster election the two pro-Ireland parties won nine MPs; the Democratic Unionists gained five seats and other unionists won three; and the Alliance Party took one MP. In keeping with the tradition of the Irish Republican Army, Sinn Fein does not recognise the Westminster parliament as the legitimate government of Northern Ireland. Thus, its candidates winning a constituency refuse to take their seats at Westminster, because it would require swearing an oath of allegiance to the Crown. This has reduced the number of MPs sitting in the 2024 UK Parliament to 643 and the size of an absolute majority to 322 MPs. The second-largest Irish party, the Social Democratic and Labour Party, has informal ties with Labour MPs, some of whom support Irish unity. Since the 18 Northern Ireland seats in the House of Commons are divided between up to six different parties, it is only in very limited circumstances that their votes could influence British government. The more important Irish vote is in cities such as Glasgow and Liverpool, where there are concentrations of voters whose families have roots in Ireland North or South.

Parties wanting to maintain the United Kingdom have always won a majority of the Westminster vote in all parts of the UK. However, the vagaries of the first-past-the-post electoral system and the division of pro-UK parties have often enabled a single nationalist party to win lots of seats with a minority of the vote. The SNP won all of its Westminster seats at the 2024 election with less than half the constituency vote. Plaid Cymru took two of its four seats with less than two-fifths of the vote. In Northern Ireland, a combination of unionist parties took more than half the vote at the 2024 election, while the two pro-Ireland parties took 38 per cent of the vote there. Reform UK's growth in support in Wales and Scotland further divides the pro-UK vote, and its attack on the shortcomings of both governing parties benefits the nationalist parties.

Since English constituencies collectively return five-sixths of all MPs, in principle a party could win control of British government even if it failed to win any MPs in Scotland, Wales or Northern Ireland. However, it would need to win 60 per cent of English seats in order to have an absolute majority in the UK House of Commons. Sir Keir Starmer's landslide victory in 2024 was big enough to give Labour such a majority. This was only the fourth time since 1950 in which a party won enough seats in England to give it an absolute majority in the United Kingdom parliament.

No limit to fourth-force parties

To start a new political party that can have an impact on the next general election requires having distinctive issues, a leader who can articulate this appeal and a few MPs, whether defectors from an established party or winners of by-elections. Otherwise, decades may be spent in fruitless discussions in online and committee debates ignored by voters and by Westminster.

At the 2024 general election the nucleus of a Muslim party was created by the unprecedented success of four Muslim candidates defeating Labour MPs in Midlands constituencies with large Muslim populations. In addition, independent Muslim candidates turned Labour seats with large Muslim populations into marginal seats. For example, Wes Streeting held Ilford North but his vote fell by 20 percentage points, and Jess Phillips's vote dropped 26 percentage points in Birmingham Yardley. Labour also lost seats to other parties due to pro-Palestine candidates hiving off a portion of Labour's vote. Although they did not campaign as a party, these Muslim candidates had a common platform: defending Palestinians against Israeli attacks in Gaza.

The four Muslim independents along with Jeremy Corbyn registered a group in Parliament in September 2024. It endorsed left-wing domestic and developing country policies that Corbyn had long supported as well as supporting Palestinians. While the alliance is not a political party, House of Commons procedures give its members more opportunities to participate in House of Commons activities. In terms of personnel, the group was Muslim; in terms of policies, it was an extension of left-wing views held by dozens of Labour MPs.

Given several dozen constituencies with substantial concentrations of Muslim voters, events in Israel and Palestine and potentially in the Indian sub-continent could give an opening for more such candidates to contest select seats. Doing so as independents requires far fewer resources than creating an organisation to field candidates contesting constituencies nationwide. Moreover, not forming a party avoids the conflict that can be generated by the need for a party to agree a programme on non-ethnic issues, such as gender, as well as clashes of opinion and ambition about who should be the leader.

The seeds for a new left-wing party were planted in the previous Parliament by Keir Starmer expelling the former Labour leader, Jeremy Corbyn. Corbyn comfortably won re-election as an independent in Islington North with a bigger share of his constituency vote than Starmer won in the neighbouring Holborn & St Pancras constituency. In the first month of the current Parliament Keir Starmer followed a tough disciplinary policy, suspending seven left-wing MPs who voted against the Labour whip to support an SNP motion to scrap the two-child benefit cap. While some of the suspended MPs were later re-admitted to Labour's ranks as part of the Starmer government's U-turn on the issue, others were not. One expelled MP, Zarah Sultana, briefly became a member of the independent group.

In response to the priority the Starmer government gave to fiscal responsibility and its avoidance of socialist policies and rhetoric, left-wing activists began discussing the formation of a new party early in the life of the Starmer government. They differed in giving priority to anti-capitalist, anti-Zionist and transgender policies (Jeffery, 2025). They also differed in their views on organisation and leadership.

Plans for a new left party went prematurely public in July 2025 when Zarah Sultana announced the formation of Your Party with Jeremy Corbyn and herself as co-leaders. Corbyn publicly declared that he had not endorsed her statement. Separate public statements made clear they differed in both style and substance.

Corbyn maintained an inclusive attitude towards different left-wing views, a policy that had enabled him to be elected leader of the Labour Party. Sultana emphasised absolute principles such as the nationalisation of the whole economy, uncritical support of Palestine, and transgender rights.

The Your Party movement registered with the Electoral Commission as a political party in September 2025 with Jeremy Corbyn named as leader. Zarah Sultana established a website to recruit paying members to the new group. It quickly raised £800,000, said to be needed to finance a founding conference. A dispute arose when Corbyn's group asked Sultana to send it funds to finance the founding conference of the new party. Two Muslim MPs who had initially associated with Your Party resigned over what they described as intolerance of their socially conservative views and slurs against Muslims. In the House of Commons list of parties, Sultana is named as the sole Your Party MP.

The party's founding conference in Liverpool on 29–30 November opened with Jeremy Corbyn and Zarah Sultana holding separate rallies. Sultana conducted a well-publicised boycott of the first day's proceedings, protesting against the exclusion from the conference of people maintaining dual membership in Your Party and in the Socialist Workers Party, a Trotskyite organisation, and the Revolutionary Communist Group. It closed with a series of contested ballots confirming that dual-party membership was acceptable. To resolve the conflict between having Corbyn as leader or a dual leadership of Corbyn and Sultana, the conference voted to give leadership to a three-person national executive, none of whom could be members of Parliament (Kenyon, 2025).

Polls were quick to ask about popular support before Your Party was legally registered. Up to 18 per cent of respondents disaffected with the direction of the Starmer government said they would consider voting for a new Corbyn-led party. Once the party was formally established and quarrels about its direction were publicised, support dropped to around 5 per cent or less. Since the conference, poll results are hypothetical not only because no election is being held but also because it is unclear whether the group now controlling Your Party will nominate six hundred candidates to fight a general election with an inclusive appeal favoured by Corbyn or an exclusive ideology favoured by Sultana. Given this uncertainty, in reporting opinion poll results this book classifies Your Party as an Other party.

The existence of a group of pro-Gaza Muslim councillors with left-wing economic views and socially conservative principles shows that the number of fourth-force parties can be expanded. For example, at the 2024 election, the Workers Party of Britain, under the leadership of pro-Palestine MP George Galloway, fought 152 seats, averaging 1,381 votes per constituency. While Galloway lost his seat in the Commons, 27 candidates saved their deposits and the party came close to defeating two Labour MPs in Birmingham.

The division among fourth-force parties covers religion, nationalism and climate change as well as substantial differences about the interpretation of socialism, ranging from sectarian Marxist views to the view of the vote-winning Labour pioneer Herbert Morrison: 'Socialism is what the Labour government does.' As long as there is no third party on the right, the fragmentation in the left vote helps Reform UK's chances of winning seats in Parliament.

Citations

Jeffery, Max, 2025. 'Inside Britain's socialist dogfight', *The Spectator*, 15 October.

Kenyon, Megan, 2025. 'The left's loveless marriage: Your Party's first conference', *New Statesman*, 5–11 December.

Larner, Jac, 2025. 'Consolidation not convergence: understanding Wales's ongoing realignment', 18 December, https://blogs.cardiff.ac.uk/thinking-wales/consolidation-not-conversion-understanding-waless-ongoing-realignment/. Accessed 21 December 2025.

Wheeler, Caroline, 2025. 'Greens "open to pacts" to keep Reform and Tories out of power', *The Times*, 28 September.

Wikipedia, 2025. https://en.wikipedia.org/wiki/Opinion_polling_for_the_next_United_Kingdom_general_election#Seat_projections_(MRP_polls). Accessed 21 December 2025.

Part III

Where will we be at the next election?

9

2029: Many scenarios, different odds

The disruption of the three-party system at the 2024 general election means that general elections are no longer general and there will also be disruption at the 2029 election. This will be the case whether there is a reversion to the hybrid three-party system prevailing between 1970 and 2019 or Reform UK has joined the Labour and Conservative Parties as a party competing for control of British government. Disruption will sever the link between constituency and national votes.

Many scenarios are possible about the party winning the most seats at the next election. This does not mean that all scenarios are equally likely. Normally, the governing party would be the odds-on favourite to win re-election, especially one with as massive a parliamentary majority as Labour secured at the 2024 election. However, because its share of the national vote was the lowest in history for any party winning a parliamentary majority, its lead rests on very thin ice. A party that won only five MPs would normally be ignored. However, Reform UK's front-running position in this Parliament's polls cannot be ignored. Any list of possible outcomes must also include a reference to what statisticians call the error term, that is, a scenario that is not accounted for in the analysis of available data.

Opinion polls can no longer be relied upon to predict the election outcome because they represent national opinion, whereas the election outcome is the sum of the results of party competition in 650 constituencies. At the constituency level, the MP defending a particular seat may belong to any one of a dozen different parties. Similarly, the party in second place is more likely to come from one of a number of non-governing parties than from the Labour or Conservative Party. Moreover, the first-past-the-post system treats very unequally parties with similar shares of the national vote. At the 2024 election the Liberal Democrats won 11 per cent of the seats in the House of Commons with 12 per cent of the national vote, whereas Reform UK won fewer than 1 per cent of Commons seats with 14 per cent of the vote.

Election-night television shows the importance of adding up results from 650 different constituencies in order to determine which party wins control of government. Coming first in an election requires a party to win seats in hundreds of constituencies that differ in how six parties compete (see Table 4.3). Winning control of government requires a party to come first in 326 politically diverse constituencies.

A statistical technique, multi-level regression and post-stratification analysis (MRP), can predict a national election outcome as the sum of predictions of the result in each of 650 constituencies. It does this by applying sample survey findings about how different social groups vote to data about the socio-economic and political characteristics of each constituency, such as its number of pensioners and unemployed (see Wikipedia, 2025, for mathematical formulae). Opinion polls that interview only a dozen or so respondents in each of about one-fifth of the country's constituencies cannot provide such detailed predictions.

Since the detailed survey data necessary to produce a credible MRP prediction requires many thousands of respondents, predictions are produced only infrequently. Five predictions have been produced by members of the British Polling Council since the Labour government passed its first anniversary on 4 July 2025 (Table 9.1). Both survey data and statistical procedures vary to a degree between predicting institutions. Thus, findings common to a number of MRP analyses provide a better indication of what could happen if a general election were held today.

If a general election were held today six conclusions are robust:

- Reform UK would come first in seats. Predictions differ about whether Reform would win a majority or a plurality of MPs.
- Labour would lose hundreds of MPs, leaving it second in seats to Reform, even if it fell to third in votes.
- Conservatives would lose up to half or more of their seats, and are at risk of finishing fourth, not third, in seats.
- The Liberal Democrats are unlikely to see a big change up or down in their seats.

Table 9.1 MRP predictions of a 2025 general election outcome

	Green	Lab.	LD	Con.	Ref.	SNP
Electoral Calculus 25 December	17	107	68	99	277	44
YouGov 24 September	7	144	78	45	311	37
Stonehaven 18 September	3	144	65	39	349	28
More in Common 15 September	9	85	35	70	381	40
Survation 1 September	6	191	63	42	293	30
Mean	8	134	62	59	322	36
General election 4 July 2024	4	411	72	121	5	9

Source: Seats of Other parties are omitted. Pack, Mark, 2025. 'Latest voting intention and leadership ratings opinion polls', www.markpack.org.uk/155623/voting-intention-opinion-poll-scorecard/. Wikipedia, 2025. 'Multilevel regression with poststratification', https://en.wikipedia.org/wiki/Multilevel_regression_with_poststratification

- The Scottish National Party will win a big majority of Scotland's 57 seats, which could make it a significant player in a hung parliament.
- The Green vote is rising but, as the biggest victim of the first-past-the-post system, it would win few seats.

MRP results, like opinion polls, are counter-factual statements measuring what would be likely to happen were a general election held at the time a prediction is made. Nonetheless, they give a more up-to-date indication of each party's current standing than the 2024 general election result, which is now an out-of-date fact. Moreover, consistent with the bias of the first-past-the-post electoral system, MRP analyses show that a 1 per cent change in a party's position in the polls can make more than a 1 per cent change in its House of Commons strength for better or for worse. All the predictions show that the next election is likely to give Reform and the SNP a bigger share of MPs than their share of the national vote and the Conservatives and Greens will get a smaller percentage of seats than votes. While the electoral system will not penalise the Labour government in the allocation of seats, the electorate is primed to do so.

9.1 Scenarios of winning control of government

MRP analyses are valuable for assessing the parliamentary strength of individual parties, they do not address which party will take control of government. This is a particular limitation when no party is predicted to win an absolute majority of seats. Nine scenarios are set out below of how a government could be formed after the next election, depending on the distribution of seats among parties, ideological constraints on co-operation and the ambitions of party leaders. Considering a variety of scenarios, some of which are mind-stretching, is particularly useful for understanding a disrupted party system in which a hung parliament is more likely than at any time for almost a century.

Manageable disruption

- Scenario 1 *A single-party majority government.* This outcome depends on the first-past-the-post electoral system manufacturing a parliamentary majority for the party with a sufficient plurality of votes. Keir Starmer benefited when Labour won a massive parliamentary majority thanks to opposition parties collectively dividing 66 per cent of the vote. For Labour to win an absolute majority it would need to increase its December 2025 standing in the polls by more than half. Likewise, for the Conservatives to win a parliamentary majority, they would need to increase their poll support by more than half, a bigger gain than that of Margaret Thatcher when she won the 1979 election. Current polls show Reform UK consistently in the lead in votes but not consistently predicted to win a majority of seats.
- Scenario 2 *A single-party minority government.* A party that wins a substantial plurality of MPs but falls just short of a majority may hold office by a deal with another party ensuring it the majority needed to win a vote of confidence. After the Labour government lost its majority during the 1974–79 Parliament it received such support from Liberal Democrat and Scottish National Party MPs in exchange for the government introducing a devolution Act of Parliament. In the 2017 Parliament, when the Conservative government of Theresa May was nine seats short of an absolute majority, it negotiated support from the Democratic Unionist Party of Northern Ireland. When that agreement broke down in 2019, her successor, Boris Johnson, called a

general election and won a parliamentary majority. In short, a single-party minority government can last indefinitely but is constantly vulnerable to defeat.

Since it does not want to participate in British government, the Scottish National Party is an ideal partner for a party that wants to govern on its own but falls dozens of seats short of a majority. The SNP's price would be an Act of Parliament transferring the right to call an independence referendum from the Westminster Parliament to the Scottish Parliament. That would put the SNP in a similar position to Sinn Fein in Northern Ireland. It could call a referendum making Scotland independent as and when opinion polls and its own political nous indicated it would win.

- Scenario 3 A *penny-farthing majority coalition* would be a two-party government in which one party is the big wheel and the other tags along behind as on a late nineteenth-century bicycle. If the Liberal Democrats could keep the 72 seats they won in the last election, their MPs would be sufficient to provide a majority to a party winning at least 254 MPs. The prospect of joining a coalition government would face Liberal Democrat leaders with a quandary. There is the attraction of gaining seats in Cabinet and sponsoring legislation. But joining a coalition with the Conservatives after the 2010 election led the Liberal Democrats to electoral disaster five years later. There are no ideological barriers to the Liberal Democrats joining a coalition with the Labour Party. However, this opportunity would arise only if Labour lost upwards of 150 seats, making it an electorally unattractive partner.

- Scenario 4 *A tricycle majority coalition.* Three parties is probably the maximum number that might workably collaborate in government. The Labour, Liberal Democrat and Green Parties are close enough ideologically to form a three-party coalition if a penny-farthing coalition fell a few seats short of a parliamentary majority and the Greens were exceptionally successful in winning seats. This could happen only if Labour made a big enough recovery from its mid-term slump to add more than a hundred MPs to its predicted amount at the beginning of 2026.
- Scenario 5 *A pogo-stick majority.* A governing party does not need to rely on the same parties to maintain control of government. It can win votes of confidence by jumping from one party to another for support, depending on the issue at hand. A majority may be obtained by including clauses in a bill to benefit a particular fourth-force party, which could sometimes be nationalist, sometimes Green or sometimes Liberal Democrat. In Norway after the September 2025 election, the Labour Party formed a government with only 31 per cent of seats in Parliament. It relies on the ad hoc votes of red and green parties for parliamentary majorities on legislation in what is described as a tutti-frutti coalition.

Disruption intensified

The above scenarios, in which either the Labour or Conservative Party forms a government, are consistent with the maintenance of a hybrid three-party system or its expansion into a four-party system if the Green Party were to become relevant in votes and seats. But what if the result of the next general election required coming to terms with Reform UK, the party of Nigel Farage? If Reform were to win enough seats so that neither Labour nor the Conservatives win enough MPs to take charge of government on lines set out above, the disruption would intensify.

- Scenario 6 *A one-party Reform UK government.* If Reform were to win an absolute majority of seats, the Labour government would have to resign promptly, and the King would be bound to ask Nigel Farage to form a government. This would give Farage the problem of doing so (see chapter 7). The party would lack the cadres of experienced MPs to fill the scores of ministerial posts that enable a governing party to give direction to government. It would only have a handful of politicians with House of Commons experience. While a Reform government with an absolute majority could survive a confidence vote, inexperienced Cabinet ministers fresh to the ways of Westminster and Whitehall could fall like ninepins in debate and votes on their ministerial behaviour. Farage could recruit people from outside Westminster and give them seats in the House of Lords but a junior minister would also be needed to answer for the department in the House of Commons. An alternative is that Farage offered ministerial posts to experienced MPs in other parties who would prefer to be ministers in a Reform government here and now rather than spend years on the Opposition benches waiting for something to turn up.

In a disrupted system of government, the seats of the three leading parties – Labour, Conservative and Reform UK – could be so divided that a majority government could be formed only if two of the parties agreed to be partners in a coalition. In simple arithmetic terms, there could be three different pairs of parties that could form a majority coalition. However, political arithmetic is never as straightforward as the arithmetic taught in school.

• Scenario 7 *A coalition of Reform UK and the Conservative Party.* If Reform came first in seats but fell short of a parliamentary majority, a coalition government of Reform and the Conservatives could negotiate an agreement on common policies. The bulk of Reform voters are ex-Conservative voters, and Conservative voters are much closer to Reform in their political outlook than to Labour. However, for the Conservatives to become junior partners of Reform would threaten the Conservatives with losing their independent standing, as the National Liberals did in partnering under Conservative leadership between the two world wars. Moreover, Nigel Farage has stated that his aim is to destroy the Conservative Party rather than partner with it. If a revived Conservative Party were to take the lead in a coalition government, having Farage as deputy prime minister would make a Conservative prime minister uncomfortable.

• Scenario 8 *A coalition of the Labour and Conservative Parties to keep Reform UK out of office.* Prime Minister Keir Starmer has described Reform UK as threatening the soul of the nation, and the Conservative leader Kemi Badenoch also talks about Reform UK as an unacceptable far-right party that should not form a government. The labelling of Reform as beyond the pale would leave a Labour–Conservative coalition as the only possible government with a parliamentary majority. Such a coalition governed Britain during the Second World War. In peacetime it would be a cartel in which party leaders combined to keep out Reform. This would play to Farage's populist claim that the Labour and Conservative Parties are united in wanting to perpetuate their hold on office. More than that, it would require Labour to lose fewer seats and the Tories to win more seats than they are credited with in the predictions in Table 9.1.

• Scenario 9 *Another roll of the dice*. Today, Reform UK is currently the party best placed to win an absolute majority at a second election by campaigning with the slogan 'Give us the votes to finish the job'. If a new government could not be formed after the 2029 election because of political obstacles, a caretaker Labour government would remain in office until a second election could be held. In October 1974 a second election turned a minority Labour government into a government with enough MPs for it to remain in office for more than four years. Neither of the two traditional governing parties is well placed to win a majority.

If rolling the dice in a second election again produced a distribution of seats such that no government could be formed with a stable coalition majority, something radical would have to be done. At that point both the Liberal Democrats and the Reform Party would give the same answer: introduce proportional representation. The Greens and the nationalist parties also support such a change. Twice-defeated Conservative and Labour Parties would have a choice between coming up with an alternative way of forming a government or ending disruptive elections by abstaining on a vote to introduce some form of proportional representation. Introducing proportional representation would create a new British party system in which coalition government would be normal, and the disruption of the party system begun by the 2024 general election would be complete.

Citations

Electoral Calculus, 2025. 'General election prediction', www.electoralcalculus.co.uk/prediction_main.html. Accessed 21 December 2025.

Pack, Mark, 2025. 'Latest voting intention and leadership ratings opinion polls', www.markpack.org.uk/155623/voting-intention-opinion-poll-scorecard/. Accessed 21 December 2025.

Wikipedia, 2025. 'Multilevel regression with poststratification', https://en.wikipedia.org/wiki/Multilevel_regression_with_poststratification. Accessed 21 December 2025.

Appendix: Sources for analysis

A book that covers three-quarters of a century must selectively present its evidence or collapse under an unbearable weight of detail. Readers can conveniently find lots of details in the sources cited below, and the internet can provide updating beyond this book's completion in early 2026.

Electoral institutions. Research Briefings published by the House of Commons Library provide authoritative expositions of the many laws and institutions involved in the conduct of United Kingdom elections and are frequently updated. In addition, the Briefings provide background information about topics being debated in Parliament and the media: researchbriefings.parliament.uk/. The Electoral Commission is the official body charged with overseeing the conduct of elections and party finance, and its website gives detailed information about topics within its terms of reference: electoralcommission.org.uk/. Because they serve the interests of all parties, the Library and the Commission give a high priority to accuracy and impartiality.

Election results. The definitive text of election results was initially compiled and published by the late F. W. S. Craig as *British Electoral Facts, 1832–1987* (Aldershot: Dartmouth, 1985) and related volumes summarised therein. Its contents were updated by Colin Rallings and Michael Thrasher in *British Electoral Facts, 1832–2012* (London: Biteback Publishing, 2012). Further updating is found in Richard Cracknell, Elise Uberoi and Matthew Burton, *UK Election Statistics: 1918–2023, A Long Century of Elections* (London: House of Commons Research Briefing, 2023). These are the primary sources of this book's election data.

Public opinion. Surveys of voting intention are published frequently in the media. Firms that are members of the British Polling Council are bound by its rules to post full technical details of published surveys on their website within two days of initial release. Wikipedia provides a continuously updated list of voting intention surveys and related data: wikipedia.org/wiki/Opinion_polling_for_the_next_United_Kingdom_general_election. An updated compilation of voting surveys also appears in theweekinpolls@substack.com along with additional data and commentary by Dr Mark Pack.

The Gallup Poll pioneered voting intention surveys; a detailed historical record can be found in Anthony King and Robert J. Wybrow, *British Public Opinion 1937–2000: The Gallup Polls* (London: Politico, 2001). The Political Monitor of Ipsos (formerly MORI) regularly updates its surveys of voting intention begun in the 1970s: ipsos.com/en-uk/uk-opinion-pollstrend. YouGov was founded in the year 2000 and conducts frequent internet surveys of voting intentions: yougov.co.uk/topics/politics/trackers/voting-intention.

The British Election Study has conducted lengthy academic surveys of political attitudes and voting at every election since 1964: britishelectionstudy.com/about/. It thus complements the focus on constituency competition for seats and control of government in a disrupted party system that is the subject of this book.

Seat predictions. National sample surveys of public opinion are insufficient to predict an electoral outcome determined by first-past-the-post results in 650 constituencies. MRP (multi-level regression with post-stratification) analysis combines very large sample surveys with detailed political, economic and social constituency data to predict the result in each of the UK's 650 constituencies and thus the hypothetical distribution of seats in the House of Commons. The sum of MRP results in Table 9.1 is updated monthly by Electoral Calculus, and I write a commentary on its significance for the control of government: electoralcalculus.co.uk/homepage.html.

Appendix

Appendix Table 1 Party vote 1950–2024 (%)

Year	Con	Lab	Lib Dem	Other
1950	43.4	46.1	9.1	1.4
1951	48.0	48.8	2.6	0.7
1955	49.7	46.4	2.7	1.2
1959	49.4	43.8	5.9	1.0
1964	43.4	44.1	11.2	1.3
1966	41.9	48.0	8.5	1.6
1970	46.4	43.1	7.5	3.1
Feb 1974	37.9	37.2	19.3	5.7
Oct 1974	35.8	39.3	18.3	6.5
1979	43.9	36.9	13.8	5.3
1983	42.4	27.6	25.4	4.6
1987	42.3	30.8	22.6	4.3
1992	41.9	34.4	17.8	5.8
1997	30.7	43.2	16.8	9.3
2001	31.6	40.7	18.3	9.4
2005	32.4	35.2	22.0	10.4
2010	36.1	29.0	23.0	11.9
2015	36.8	30.4	7.9	24.8
2017	42.3	40.0	7.4	10.3
2019	43.6	32.1	11.5	12.8
2024	23.7	33.7	12.2	30.4

Sources: 1950–2019: https://researchbriefings.files.parliament.uk/documents/CBP-7529/CBP-7529.pdf#page=8; 2024: https://researchbriefings.files.parliament.uk/documents/CBP-10009/CBP-10009.pdf

Appendix Table 2 Party seats in the House of Commons 1950–2024

Year	Con	Lab	Lib Dem	Other
1950	298	315	9	3
1951	321	295	6	3
1955	345	277	6	2
1959	365	258	6	1
1964	304	317	9	0
1966	253	364	12	1
1970	330	288	6	6
Feb 1974	297	301	14	23
Oct 1974	277	319	13	26
1979	339	269	11	16
1983	397	209	23	21
1987	376	229	22	23
1992	336	271	20	24
1997	165	418	46	30
2001	166	412	52	29
2005	198	355	62	31
2010	306	258	57	29
2015	330	232	8	80
2017	317	262	12	59
2019	365	202	11	72
2024	121	411	72	46

Sources: 1950–2019: https://researchbriefings.files.parliament.uk/documents/CBP-7529/CBP-7529.pdf#page=8; 2024: https://researchbriefings.files.parliament.uk/documents/CBP-10009/CBP-10009.pdf

Appendix Table 3 Monthly average of polls since 2024 election (%)

	Lab	Con	Reform	Lib Dem	Green
General election popular vote	34.7	24.4	14.7	12.6	6.9
Jul 2024	35.7	21.0	16.3	11.0	8.3
Aug 2024	34.3	23.8	16.9	11.7	6.8
Sep 2024	31.0	24.0	17.8	13.2	7.4
Oct 2024	29.5	25.2	18.8	12.7	7.3
Nov 2024	27.7	26.7	19.3	12.2	7.7
Dec 2024	27.5	24.6	21.6	11.7	8.1
Jan 2025	25.8	23.8	23.9	12.1	8.3
Feb 2025	25.1	21.9	25.7	12.8	8.4
Mar 2025	25.1	22.6	24.5	13.1	8.7
Apr 2025	23.8	21.6	25.3	13.9	9.0
May 2025	22.7	18.0	29.9	14.1	9.4
Jun 2025	23.3	18.5	28.9	13.7	9.2
Jul 2025	22.6	17.9	29.4	14.1	9.3
Aug 2025	21.1	17.8	30.3	13.5	8.8
Sep 2025	20.9	17.5	31.1	13.2	9.8
Oct 2025	19.4	17.5	30.9	13.2	12.3
Nov 2025	19.1	18.5	29.6	13.6	13.6
Dec 2025	17.8	19.4	28.8	12.8	14.7

Notes: Average calculated for all polls with fieldwork commencing in a given month. The general election result is for Great Britain rather than the UK because polls normally do not interview in Northern Ireland.
Source: PollBase, www.markpack.org.uk/opinion-polls/

Index

Index

Index